THE CHALLENGE OF MARRIAGE

There is nothing more beautiful than a solid and meaningful love.

Timeless counsel and wisdom by

Bob Garon

First printing 1991

Published by VGV PUBLICATIONS

Printed in the United States of America.

Cover layout and internal formatting: Francisca de Zwager

For information: P.O Box MCPO 2099
Sen Gil Puyat Avenue, Makati City, Philippines, 1260
or www.facebook.com/bobgaron

ISBN: 978-1-7378277-2-6

Royalties earned from this book will help poor children in the Philippines get an education.

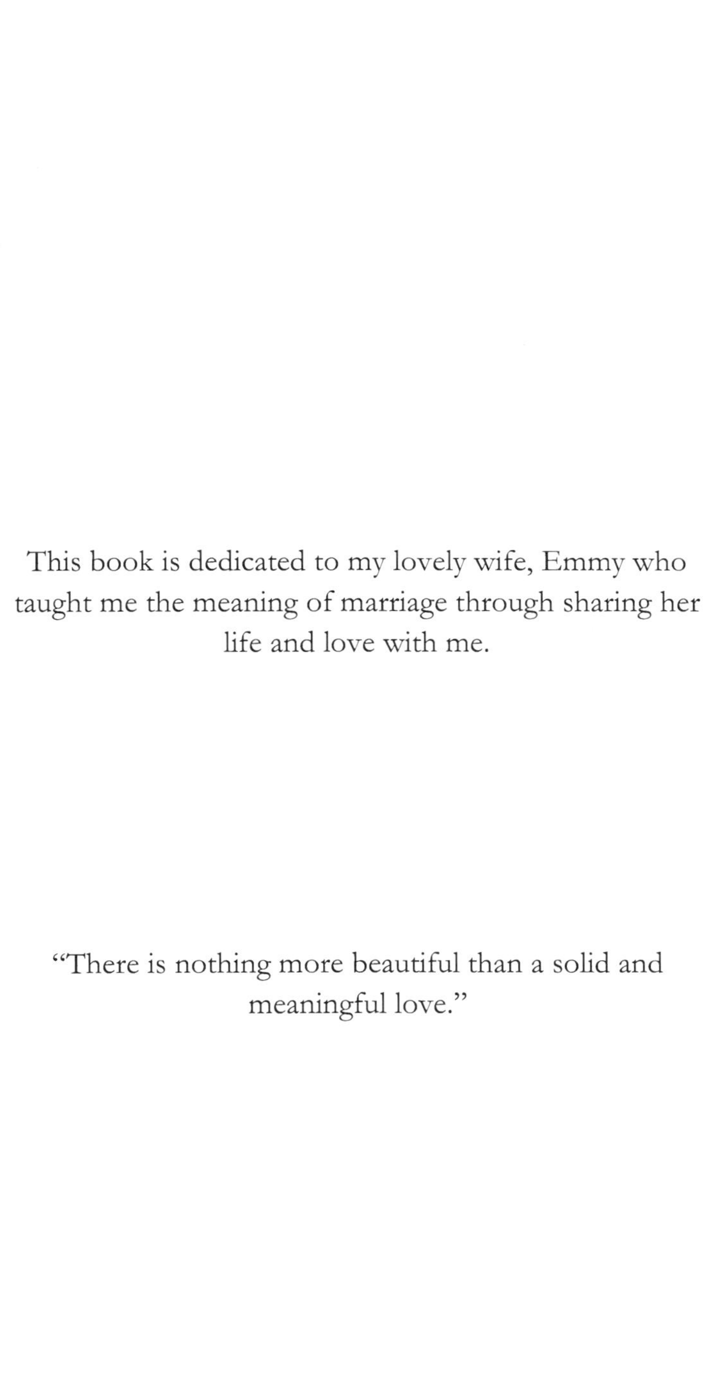

This book is dedicated to my lovely wife, Emmy who taught me the meaning of marriage through sharing her life and love with me.

"There is nothing more beautiful than a solid and meaningful love."

Contents

Foreword

I grew up hearing my father tell us, "One of the most important decisions you will ever make is who you will marry." He would often say that the choice of a partner could make or break the rest of your life. And as I look back at the incredible years he and my mother lived, what they made together, and people they helped, I couldn't agree more.

My dad would say that a relationship is a living, breathing thing. You can turn your back on it for a while only to discover it started to wilt from your inattention. If you don't notice and correct it early enough, it may be too late by the time something unwanted happens. You can also focus on it so deeply for it to bring out the best not only in you and your partner but also in your children and the people around you. He believed his marriage lasted 44 years, and they grew more deeply in love with each passing day, because he and my mom lived as if anytime the relationship could go wrong. Not to the point of being overly fearful, but they were keenly aware of the traps in marriage and what he liked to call "marital drift," which could happen anytime. Once drifting apart happens, it can be hard to come back together. So, everything they did in their relationship was done thoughtfully and with careful deliberation. I don't think I have ever seen two people as in sync as my parents.

This book is a compilation of my dad's newspaper column articles written in the late 1970's up to the early 1980's where he shared his advice on the challenges of marriage and relationships. Sometimes, people would write him with problems and questions, and he would share his perspective on what makes a marriage work. His unique take on loving solutions, such as their love book (a personal book he and my mother wrote in to express their love for each other), morning wrap-arounds (morning hugs he would share with mom), and everything in between, is found in his writings.

In his spirit, I say take what is useful and leave behind what you don't need. I grew up with his voice on the important topic of marriage and I find myself benefitting from that now as a wife and a mother. I hope, like me, you will take away something valuable from this book and bring it into your relationship with your partner.

Alexandra Garon-Mañosa
(Manila, 2022)

A DEEP AND MEANINGFUL RELATIONSHIP

WE HEAR SO MUCH about unhappy marriages and broken homes. This is an age when divorces and separation are as common as the rising and the setting of the sun. Men fooling around or coming home drunk while the woman weep. Unhappy couples who feel that they would have been far better off if they had never married.

It is indeed refreshing to run into couples whose lives are deeply meaningful because of the love and affection they have for one another. These spouses inspire us and cause us to keep faith in the institution of marriage.

I remember one such couple. My cousin Priscilla and her husband, Arthur. Ever since I was a teener, I can remember them as a harmonious couple who always got along well and whose love was sparkling and vibrant. I cannot remember ever getting the feeling or impression that they were angry or disappointed with each other.

Quite the contrary. The way they loved was like telling the world that they were the luckiest couple in the world.

Just a few weeks ago, Arthur died. He had fought a brave but losing battle against cancer. Priscilla wrote a letter that is deeply touching. It reflects her strong love for her man. More than that, it speaks of the pain of losing a beloved. Most inspiring, it tells of a woman's determination to go on living in spite of her loss. I know she will not mind if I share with you some excerpts of her letter:

"I've dreaded having to tell you this. Arthur died last Monday (the 3rd) morning. The funeral was Thursday, the 6th."

"Claudia and her family had flown back home on Friday. We did have wonderful Holidays. He seemed so happy that we were all together. In fact, we had a quiet New Year's Eve with Burks. We had dinner and played bridge. On New Year's Day, he had difficulty breathing and had to use oxygen more than usual. We contacted the doctor Sunday morning and one of the clinic doctors came to the house, examined him and diagnosed pneumonia and made arrangements for an ambulance. He was truly wonderful, a caring man, a God-send in a crisis."

"The end was very peaceful, exactly what he wanted. He just stopped breathing. He was in the hospital only 12 hours. I'll be forever grateful that he was home with me till the end. Dr. Gerken confessed that when she first examined him, she gave him six months. She's amazed that he survived almost two years."

"Claudia flew back Monday night. I've been blessed with such wonderful children. Charlies and Liz had four-month-old Sarah here with them and her presence helped so much to alleviate the sadness. Nothing can destroy our beautiful memories. We had 36 wonderful years. I read once that the quality of a man's life is measured by how deeply he has touched the lives of others and Arthurs was such a special person. The thought of life without him is unbearable, but I don't have much choice. Everyone has been very kind and attentive, but in the final analysis, it's my ability to accept and cope that I have to deal with. Please pray for me."

PERFECT LOVE MEANS COMPLETE SHARING

THE OTHER DAY I was talking to a married man who had such a big problem that he had to resort to all sorts of tranquilizers to cut down his intense tension. When I asked him if he had shared his difficulty with his wife, he said he had not because "she would only worry about it, and besides she would not really understand."

It's a well-known fact that many married couples do not share as much as they would like people to think they do. There is a lot of hide-and-seek going on in countless homes. Husbands and wives are often excellent players of the famous cat-and-mouse game.

In many homes, the reason for hiding things is not because one of the partners is fooling around. Often it is a sincere concern for marital harmony and the intense desire to safeguard love that keeps couples from being frank and honest.

How often have I heard a wife tell me: "Bob, I never talk about this subject because it really upsets my husband so very much." Or the husband says: "Whenever I bring up this matter she gets hurt, so I just keep silent."

I am not suggesting that this is a totally bad thing to do. Sometimes it is better to be silent than to alienate each other more deeply. Silence is often the lesser of two evils. Many couples are able to preserve an apparent harmony and by not breaking the "peace" they still have fine moments and share in life's joy and sorrows. However, in the process, they are growing farther and farther apart and are becoming more strangers to one another. Real dialogue becomes increasingly difficult.

Because of the growing fear to "say the wrong thing," there is less and less meaningful communication. Finally, the two suddenly find themselves completely alienated. When that happens, the end is just around the corner.

Paul Tournier, the distinguished marriage counselor, once wrote. "It's always a denial of love, and to some extent a disavowal of marriage, to begin to calculate what one says does not say, even when it is done with the excellent motive of safeguarding one's love. It is a contradiction of the law of marriage instituted by God: "They are no more twain, but one flesh' (Matt. 19:5)."

There is no question here, as there is in the child's relationship with his parents, of a right to keep secrets, since the marriage partner has actually been chosen freely as a privileged confidant.

I do not hesitate to say that the deeper the love, the less there is left unshared, good and bad. Ideally, perfect love means complete sharing. Easy? Of course not. That's why we call it perfect love. Yet, it's certainly worth trying because the closer to perfection one loves, the greater the rewards.

ON FALLING IN LOVE

ONE OF THE GREATEST factors that contributes to exciting living is the search for a truly understanding friend — one who is all that you have ever dreamed a true friend should be.

I said "the search" because, just as the hunter enjoys himself immensely by simply moving through the forest looking for tracks and traces of his prey, so we human beings feel our pulse rate increase whenever we sense that perhaps we have finally stumbled onto the person we think we fulfill our many and varied emotional needs.

We get all excited over merely searching for deep and meaningful friendship and love because these are not always easy to find. True love is like a precious stone. First you have to search long and hard for it. Once found, it requires hours of precision work, polishing and cutting, to make it glitter and sparkle and give its true worth.

True love is talked about so much because people do not experience it as often as one suspects. When I speak to students (male as well as female) about loving truly and deeply, they can listen for hours without end. They all have that look about them which seems to say: "I had better understand well so that I can know what went wrong in my love relationship." Or: "When I meet the one who will come into my life, I want to be sure I don't do anything stupid to mess it all up." Whenever i give a retreat to young people, I always save my talks on love, courtship, and sex for the early afternoon session. It's the only thing that keeps them awake.

All of us are always falling in love. What I mean is that we are forever meeting wonderful people who are attractive and who cause us to ask (consciously or subconsciously): "Is he the one I can fully trust with my dreams and inspirations, my secrets and the whole truth (good and bad) about myself?" We wonder if this newcomer is not the one we have been wishing for and praying to meet all these years.

We have been so disappointed so often that we almost don't care to hope or expect anything significant to come up anymore. But because, as the song says: "I don't care what they say, I won't stay in a world without love," we are willing to risk involvement again and again in the hope of finally finding that one person with whom we can really "click."

Perhaps the reason I feel so cheated when a friendship I have worked so hard to build falls down and is shattered into a million little pieces is that I have invested so much of myself—all to no avail. Besides, I've got only one life to live and it won't be that long either.

We all have an inborn, burning desire to find a true friend. Perhaps it is because true friendship and intense love imply a total acceptance of myself (the beautiful and the ugly) by someone else. And I need this because I need the assurance that I am worthwhile and lovable.

People who have never experienced deep love feel insecure, inadequate, and rejected. Is it any wonder? Nobody has ever made them feel accepted so that they go from one person to the next, afraid to really be themselves. And of course, people see their shallowness and hypocrisy and dislike them for it. Consequently, they feel more discouraged than ever.

However, no matter how often we are beaten and disappointed in love, we go on searching for that elusive true friend. Why? Because the only alternative is emotional death and madness.

NEED FOR 'COMMONNESS' IN A RELATIONSHIP

FOR A MARRIAGE or a relationship to work well, much has to happen. It is not as easy as the storybooks would have us believe. A thousand combinations of problems can occur to foul up things and upset the applecart.

One basic principle in the building of a relationship is to be sure that the right materials are present before starting construction. When a man falls in love with a woman, he is getting involved with more than just a body. That body houses a mind that has been formed over the years and espouses certain values and beliefs and convictions, some negotiable, others non-negotiable. That person comes from a religious, economic and educational background that may be totally different from his.

Like everything that needs to be built, parts must fit together. You cannot put a square peg in a round hole. The same is true of relationships. He, uneducated, uncultured, and exceedingly poor. She, educated in the best schools, having traveled the world and lived in absolute luxury all her life. If they somehow end up married, one of two things must happen. Either he moves up to her level or she will drop down to his. In either case, there will be a multitude of problems that will be almost insurmountable. Of course, there have been exceptions to the rule. However, they have been few and far between.

There needs to be some amount of "commonness" in their relationship. There must be some kind of harmony between them when it comes to background, convictions, and interests. Otherwise, there will be enormous strain put on the relationship. The pressure will be so great that an erosion of love will almost surely take place. Remember that love is a vibrant, living reality. It either grows strongly or is weakened. However, it is never static. Never! Either your love has grown today or it has gone downhill. Perhaps you have not noticed any change either way, however, there can be no doubt that it has moved in either direction ever so little. It has surely not remained the same yesterday and today.

Because of this, love is as susceptible to debilitating diseases as is the human body. Emotional stress and tensions born of conflict can ravage love. And when the differences between lovers are too great, they cause conflict. And conflict always weakens a relationship. And, a great deal of conflict puts such a strain on the infrastructure of love that soon huge cracks begin to appear in its walls. Ultimately, the pressures mount to the point where one or both parties can no longer stand up under them. When this level is reached, the end is nearing. The fewer pressures that are built-in from the beginning of a relationship, the better the chances of it succeeding.

THE HUMAN NATURE OF MAN

HE HAD BEGUN regretting that he had married her about two months after the wedding day. It wasn't because she was an evil woman. Quite the opposite. Deep in his heart he knew that she was a fine woman. He could not pinpoint the reasons for his uneasiness about her. In his heart, he felt she was not his kind of woman.

He started to play around with other women and before long he got himself involved in some messy affairs. His wife discovered him and soon his home life became full of stresses and tensions that he found difficult to bear. After a couple of years of this, he left her for another woman. After some time, his feelings for his new woman began to wane in much the same ways as before. Regret began to creep into his heart until finally he got involved with yet another girl.

This kind of happening is not unusual. In fact, it occurs in many marriages. The problem lies in the expectations of a spouse. If a man does not *really* know what he wants from a woman, he, of course, will be disappointed somehow, somewhere in the future.

I have often said that unfulfilled expectations are perhaps the greatest single factor that causes our unhappiness. This has been proven time and time again. When a woman marries, she has built up some expectations about her man, family life, her career perhaps, etc. if things do not work out the way she expected them to; if reality falls far below her expectations; then, you can be sure that she will be a disappointed and unhappy woman. If what does happen is close to her expectations, and should things work out much better than she expected, then her joy will be great.

Now, if a man (like the one above) does not have a definite concept of the kind of woman, the kind of marriage he wants, matrimony will be for him a question of his and miss. Pure chance. He will be unable to pick out the right woman for himself because he does not know what to look for. He has only a vague idea of his concept of a woman. If the right one stood in front of him, he would not recognize her. In short, he does not know what he is looking for.

This is the type of man who can never seem to be happy with a woman. Like a child in a room full of toys he plays first with one woman, then another. Never satisfied, never content, there seems to be no end to his wanderings. Such a man is dangerous to any woman who may become his wife. Unless he is able to better define what he wants in a woman, he will be condemned to a life of endless searching without finding. Like a puppy dog running around in circles, he will find himself continuously moving around aimlessly, always finding himself so near and yet so far.

THE MIND CAN BE MANIPULATED

SHE KNEW THAT he gambled a lot before they married. In fact, she had begged him many times to give it up. However, he went right on, winning sometimes but losing most of the time. She knew that she was marrying a gambler, even as they both knelt before the altar. And later on, in the financially difficult years that followed as the gambling went on unabated, she grew increasingly helpless in the face of her situation. In the end, things became so hopeless that she gave up trying to pull the family out of his gambling debts. Her love and respect for him had dissipated and, after much soul-searching, she left him.

Her love for him was not blind. It was never blind, not even for one minute. Her brain did not cease to function when she fell in love. If anything, it had worked harder scrutinizing the man she seriously considered marrying.

Many who had tried to warn her of the dire consequences of her marriage to him said that "she was crazy." others sighed and said: "love is blind; what can you do?"

Love is not blind; it merely chooses to close its eyes. Love is a feeling, but a feeling that works in tandem with the mind. A woman's mind tells her that it is good to marry. Perhaps it says that unless she marries soon, she will end up spinster for life. However, her mind (her sharp mind) also flashes warning lights when it perceives trouble. Her intellect functions all the while, presenting arguments pro and con.

However, the mind can be manipulated. It can be fooled into seeing things *this* way when reality is really *that* way. The alcoholic manipulates his own mind into arguing in favor of his continued indulgence in a pleasure that he does not *really* want to give up. In order to do this, he must come up with arguments that are convincing enough to his own intellect because we cannot live with ourselves if we don't make sense to ourselves. And so, the alcoholic argues that he needs liquor to relax; that it is important in his job that he drinks; that his friends are all drinking, etc., etc.

In like manner, the woman whose brain flashes to her signals that perhaps his man is not the right person for her must scramble to convince herself that her thinking is faulty; that there must be some mistake somewhere. And so, she begins to manipulate her own mind, cheating a little bit here and deceiving herself a bit there until in the end, she has completely fooled herself into thinking that an awful situation is really quite desirable after all.

ADJUSTMENTS IN MARRIAGE

WHEN A YOUNG MAN is courting a woman, there is something unreal about the whole thing. He likes to think that his beloved is the only girl of her kind in this vast universe of ours. She is, of course, all of that.

This knowledge gives the guy a wonderful feeling because if she is unique, then he is also unique in appreciating her and it is this uniqueness that has set him and his love apart from all other lovers and their loves.

After a couple of years of marriage (sometimes a lot sooner) his "unique" love is washing dishes, wearing curlers all too often, spending his money on things he feels are unnecessary, and nagging him on a regular schedule.

In other words, her uniqueness has slowly but surely faded away and what now remains is a woman very much like all the other women. He feels cheated and short-changed. He may even feel like kicking himself for not having made the right choice.

His wife, too, feels that things are not as she hoped they would be. The glamour and magic, the adventure and excitement of courtship have given way to the everyday dreariness and routine of household chores. She also feels that more often than before, her husband has been taking her for granted. And there are moments when she wonders if the man she married is the same person who courted her with so much courtesy and chivalry.

In other words, both are suffering from the blues of disappointment and disillusionment. It is a little bit like the first day of work after a long holiday weekend.

Most people who are at least somewhat mature can understand that this is a part of the game of life and is really to be expected.

The real problem lies in the fact that when two people (sincere, well-meaning, and truly in love) enter into a marriage, they bring with them their previous behavioral patterns and habits, both good and bad.

People don't change by kneeling at the altar of God by merely saying, "I do." True, God gives the newlyweds an abundance of grace, but this divine help works on the human in them.

A mature couple understands that marriage means lots of adjusting of attitudes and behavior on the part of both partners. When a man marries, his lifestyle necessitates changes, some of them quite radical.

The same goes for the woman. If both are willing to make the necessary adjustments, the problems that must surely arise will be worked out.

If not, then you can be sure that a lot of rough seas lie ahead.

OPENNESS BEFORE MARRIAGE

"I MARRIED YOU because I loved you and wanted to make you happy." Nothing could be farther from the truth. One does not marry to make another happy. One marries to make himself happy. Those who walked down the aisle "out of pity" for the man or because "she was pregnant and I had to save her honor" almost always found themselves in deep marital trouble soon after the honeymoon. We marry because we have needs, not simply because we want to love and cherish another person. We marry because we want a friend who will give us constant companionship. We marry because we have sexual needs that cry out for fulfillment; because we want security, children, someone we can depend on; because we have all kinds of needs that we believe can best be met through marriage.

I think that if we discuss this matter long enough, we will agree that the above statements are basically true. Yet, when courtship is going on, couples are hardly ever vocal about their needs. There is a lack of openness on this matter.

Perhaps, it is because talking about "my needs" may sound awfully selfish and might turn off my beloved. Or maybe. If I voice out my needs, I may learn that my partner cannot or is unwilling to fulfill them. If this happens, our whole courtship could be in terrible jeopardy. And since I do not want to face up to that possibility, I would rather not discuss the subject of my needs.

The fear of losing a prospective spouse is perhaps the greatest single reason for not discussing openly one's needs *before* marriage. I said *before* because, sooner or later, there *will* be a discussion. And when it does take place, it is usually under conditions of stress and tension. When needs surface and things become unbearable, then, you can be sure that both spouses will begin talking freely about them.

I think the name of the game is to talk about your needs *before* you make a lifetime commitment. In like manner, you should want to hear what your fiancé's needs are too, for you may find that you are unable or unwilling to answer them. Knowing this at an early date can save everyone a whole lot of pain.

The problem lies in the fact that we are unwilling to face possible harsh reality. And so, instead, we lull ourselves to sleep thinking that if we do not discuss such unpleasant matters, they will go away and not bother us anymore.

Not true. Marriages break up because one or both spouses feel cheated. I am disappointed because I have a host of unfulfilled expectations which I feel will never be satisfied. And it has now become clear that my partner is not the one to ever fulfill them. So, either I stay and continue to suffer, or I go somewhere else and look for someone else.

Facing up to the issue of needs early in a relationship makes a whole lot of sense. Be brave. Don't worry about rejection. You may be surprised to find out that this kind of openness is really the medicine for a courtship.

GROWTH IN A RELATIONSHIP

If there is one quality in a marriage that marks it as healthy and vital, it is the *freedom to be.* To be what? To be whatever. There are relationships that promote growth. These are the ones that have the greatest chances to succeed.

When a man takes a woman to be his wife, he does not own her. He does have certain rights over her as she has over him. However, she retains the "freedom to be" till her dying day. We all have certain inalienable rights that are God-given. One of them is to grow as a person.

There are men and women who do not see things this way. They are firmly convinced that marriage gives them rights even if they violate their beloved's freedom to be.

If the woman is willing to give up their right, then, that is privilege. She does not have to grow. If she chooses not to, then her desire should be respected. If, however, she decides to exercise her right to grow, then you can expect conflict to erupt.

When a woman feels stifled at home and wishes to pursue a career, this is her right. If her husband wants her to stay at home and tend to the children, then we run into trouble. His wishes are working at cross-purposes with hers. They conflict. And unless they can successfully negotiate their differences, there will be unhappiness.

If the woman is forced to remain at home, she does so with resentment in her heart and this bitterness stands an almost certain chance of growing more intensely as time passes. She will become angrier and angrier until someday her negative feelings spill over into the open. Then, the conflict intensifies even more.

What is necessary is for the couple to negotiate and somehow come to conclusions that will tend to the needs of both. Of course, this takes time, effort and no small degree of maturity. But it can be done. She might work part time and arrange her schedule in such a way that is acceptable to the husband. Then, she is happy and he is satisfied.

Whenever one of the partners gets it all his way all the time, there will be resentment in the other partner. And resentment, even if it is not expressed, is deadly. If not in the short term, then, its negative effect will be felt over a longer period of time.

The couples that can allow each other to meet their individual needs will reap the greatest happiness. It will also be a lasting relationship. When my needs are met by my woman, I have a little desire to go elsewhere. Also, I want to do all in my power to meet her needs and keep her happy so that she may continue to love me and make me happy. If we can keep each other satisfied by attending to our mutual needs, then, we both have every reason to exert every effort at guarding our love and not allowing it to lose its depth and its intensity.

FEELINGS DON'T THINK

THERE IS SOMETHING that I have noticed about conflict among friends and lovers. No matter how close two persons are to each other, when a conflict arises between them, it seems to them that they are drawing apart.

Take the husband and wife who are deeply in love. They disagree on an issue. Perhaps some hurting words are spoken. Hard feelings surface. Because of the opposing views which have been displayed in an offensive manner, the two spouses find that they are withdrawing into themselves. They sense that an invisible wall is building itself up between them. They somehow feel alienated from each other, to a greater or lesser degree.

They did not plan it that way. In fact, they wish things had not turned out in such a way, but the reality of the whole unpleasant episode is that their disagreement has served as a sort of wedge that has been driven between them.

We are fragile creatures who easily get hurt. Sometimes, I think that our feelings are made of glass.

That would not be dangerous if only we were ruled by our minds. But sadly, we often allow our feelings to walk all over our thinking. And that is what gets us terribly confused.

When two people in love argue and disagree, they do not love each other less. On the contrary, their disagreement may just be a strong sign of responsible concern. Perhaps the bone of contention is altogether unimportant and irrelevant. If the couple is to look at their situation rationally, there should be no question about loving each other less.

But there is. Even if they deny it. This is so because whenever we get hurt, we feel rejected. And rejection is rightly or wrongly interpreted as a sure sign of being unloved and unwanted. It may not be so in reality, but feelings do not think and cannot distinguish between what is real and what is simply imagined as real. The mind is supposed to attend to that process.

However, there are times when our feelings are so strong and making so much noise that our thinking process is simply overwhelmed and does not function the way it should.

Because of hurt feelings, we see our relationship in a distorted manner. Our thinking is so out of focus that we might even go so far as to call into question our whole relationship, which is in reality solid and meaningful.

And, when our feelings subside and fade into oblivion, we wonder why we got so absent and doubted our loved one in the first place. We might even feel embarrassed about the whole thing. A sense of guilt often follows such an irrational episode.

What we must remember, and remember well, is that *feelings don't think* and unless we are aware of this truth, we can easily make the fatal mistake of listening and ignoring what our minds are telling us.

LOVE LURES UNEXPECTING VICTIMS

IT'S SO EASY. You see the girl. She's pretty. Well built. Well dressed. Nice smile. You talk to her. She speaks well. Good conversationalist. Chooses her words carefully. Is very intelligent. Pleasant too.

Two or three days later you feel something that says "I love her." You have "fallen in love." Phew! What an experience! And what's more, she feels the same way about you.

Just about the easiest thing to do in the world is to fall in love. It's so simple. Take two people, a man and a woman. Strangers. Better still if they are both lonely and feel that nobody cares one bit.

Then bring them into close contact with each other. Allow them to communicate and reach out to one another, even on a very superficial level. Let this interaction cause the wall separating them to break down. Let them feel that closeness, that oneness that comes naturally when two people touch each other's heart. And should this feeling of intimacy lead to sexual attraction and consummation, you have one of the most exhilarating feelings any human being can ever experience. It is an almost heavenly feeling if the two people involved were previously shut off from love and isolated from people who know the art of caring for others.

This sensation of falling in love may be "out of this world" but it is tragically deceptive for countless young and old couples who daily fall victims to its lure.

"Falling in love" is so easy and so simple that most people rush into it without really suspecting that, like an interesting mystery novel where the first paragraphs are purposely written to catch the attention of the reader, the feeling of falling head over heels for somebody is strangely attractive. It's almost like floating weightlessly in space.

However, falling in love is different from "being in love" or, more technically, the "state of love." Falling in love is fantastically easy, but creating the proper atmosphere and nursing his love to maturity is something else again.

People's first impression of other people are usually misleading or downright false even if they happen to be accompanied by pleasurable feelings. Sooner or later (and it's usually sooner than later) our two lovers become well acquainted. Their closeness loses more and more of its magic until their hostilities, their disappointments, their boredom, all contribute to the elimination of that "feeling of falling in love" they earlier experienced. Then either aggressiveness begins to surface, and, before long, both are busily rebuilding the walls that had separated them.

I never cease to be amazed at the frivolity and the lack of understanding most people exhibit when approaching love. They seem so sure of themselves, so certain of success, that I wonder if they purposely refuse to look at the untold millions of broken hearts strewn about all over the world, all of them sad but undeniable testimonies to the failure of men and women to love properly.

Love lures unsuspecting victims down the road to nowhere, so often I am surprised to see great crowds of intelligent people tripping over themselves and pushing their way down the same path over and over again. Perhaps so many of us are love-starved to such a tragic extent that we are willing to charge down the same road repeatedly in the desperate hope of stumbling upon something to alleviate our cravings for somebody to fill the vast vacuum within us.

More care should be taken, more brain matter should be used when these raging passions sweep over us. Keeping things and feelings in their proper perspective has always been one of man's biggest problems. From generation to generation, he never seems to learn.

There is falling and falling. Some people know how to fall without getting hurt. Others always seem to fall flat on their faces.

TO LOVE AGAIN

THERE IS NOTHING more beautiful than a solid and meaningful love relationship. Both man and woman feel as though the world belongs to them. They feel that there is nothing they cannot do, no obstacles too great, no burdens too heavy for them because their love is so tremendous. Their happiness knows no bounds. They call themselves the luckiest people in the world.

Then, one day, the roof comes crashing down on them. Their indescribable happiness turns sour. If only they had not been so happy, then they would not now be so sad.

Like when one of the loves learns that he/she has been lied to and deceived. Then, suddenly, there is great disappointment. The tremendous letdown is followed by a feeling of having been cheated and taken for a ride.

A letter writer expressed some of these feelings when she wrote:

"I am presently employed in a private firm in the city. There I met this very aggressive man. A relationship was soon formed. He is loving and thoughtful. I see him as my ideal man. The times that we were together seemed heavenly for me. But changes occur, Bob. *Happiness can also lead to loneliness, disappointment, and a broken heart.*

"Just a few days ago, he told me that he's married and has a child. But, that information was late in coming because we have already gone to bed.

"No matter how I try to get him out of my mind, I can't do it. Especially because he tells me they are not legally married.

"I'm not talking to him, even over the phone, but I feel terrible. What are the consequences of going on with the relationship? Or putting it to an end which I cannot seem to do?"

First, let me say that she is not the first to be lied to in this way. Countless women entered into a "courtship" only to learn that the guy has a family. What worries me about this kind of thing is that the opening moments of such a relationship are born of lies and deception.

It is as if the guy is leading the woman on, like the hunter who lures his prey into a trap. Once caught, the poor victim struggles to get out, but cannot.

I also have to wonder how many other lies he told her all this time in order to cover up his marriage. I must doubt his contention that "he is not legally married." If he is not legally married, then he simply isn't married. I think that's a lot of excuses. He's leading her on again, giving her hope when he doesn't really intend to ever marry her.

If she doesn't walk away from him, she's in for a lot more pain. And, unless she can say goodbye, she will end up a mistress with no guarantees of security and forever wondering when he will take off on her.

If he really loves her and not his wife, if he isn't legally married; if he's serious about a permanent relationship; then let him leave his wife and family and "marry" her. If he cannot or will not, then she can be sure that he continues to lie to her. And, if she wishes to go on with such a man, then that's up to her. However, I would be the most surprised man in the world if it works out.

If she leaves him, she will have to deal with her disappointments, her feelings of rejection and her sense of emotional bankruptcy. However, all this is temporary. If she works at it, she can recover and love again. This time, hopefully, it will be a man who is up front with her from the beginning.

LOVE... THE SECOND TIME AROUND

WHEN A WOMAN LOSES through death a husband she has loved deeply, love the "second time around" may not at all "be better." In fact, it may be an extremely difficult experience. If a woman (the same is true of a husband who loses his wife) has had a super relationship with her man, loving again will most surely be more difficult than the first time. There are a number of reasons for this.

The first is the most obvious. Her wonderful years of marriage may be a hard act to follow. When there has been so much joy, so much harmony, there is a kind of apprehension about being able to get into a second marriage that will be as good. It is a little like being used to eating in excellent restaurants. One does not relish the thought of perhaps having to take regular meals in Nena's Eatery. The good old days of intense loving and peaceful living have created certain expectations of marriage.

The woman who has been deeply loved and given much affection and care is used to being treated this way. And she is loath to think of being dealt with any other manner. That is why she will approach her second marriage carefully and with a degree of trepidation. Will I be as happy the second time around? Will I be walking into a trap? Am I better off living alone with my children and dedicating myself to loving them? What if the next man does not love even one of my children? What then, Or, what if one of the children cannot get along with him?

These are moments when such a woman begins to believe that love and marriage the second time around may be full of all kinds of complications. These possible difficulties take some of the glitter off the prospects of a second marriage.

Then, there are the inevitable comparisons. Any man that steps into the shoes of her dead husband should expect to be compared. If a woman has had an unhappy marriage, he stands a good chance of coming out ahead. Even a little bit of happiness will constitute a big improvement over her past. If, on the other hand, her relationship with her first husband was beautiful, the second man may find all kinds of hardships when he tries to love her in his own way. When he is wanting in areas that the first husband excelled in, he will be compared. And such comparisons will most often be negative in nature. Should she begin to have regrets about marrying him, trouble will inevitably set in.

For some women, the happy memories of the past are enough to sustain their needs for the rest of their lives. Others may find it so far a while. Then, as the memories fade, their needs cry out for satisfaction. They long for companionship, affection, and love. The need for security (financial and emotional) may play a strong role.

No matter how risky these once happily married women may feel, those whose needs remain unfulfilled, will once again consider marriage. On the other hand, there are those who have experienced such an intense degree of joy and happiness in their marriage that they cannot be convinced that love will be better the second time around. The risks are so great that they prefer to do without.

DEALING WITH HURT CAUSED BY BETRAYAL

SHE WOKE UP in the middle of the night thinking about him. For more than an hour, she could not get back to sleep. She tossed and turned and remembered what he had done to her. After so much emotional investment on her part, he had casually walked away from her without explanation. She felt insulted and disgusted. How could he do such a thing? What kind of a man was he? How could he have betrayed her so callously?

Since the day of the break up, she had been having the greatest difficulty getting him out of her mind. And whenever she thought of him, it was always with bitter resentment. Every single day, it seemed that the anger in her heart kept rising in intensity. What was worse was that she could not find him in order to give him a piece of her mind. She felt like screaming at him at the top of her voice, but he was not there. She felt like pulling his hair. However, he was nowhere to be found. Her anger was like cancer eating her up inside. And there was pain. Lots of it. If her feelings could bleed, there would be blood aplenty all over the walls.

This kind of happening is neither rare nor abnormal. It happens every day to countless people. Whenever one feels betrayed by a friend or a spouse or a business associate, anger and resentment set in. You feel cheated. You have been made a fool and you know it. And this reality punches a hole into your legitimate sense of pride. You have been played with. And this thought creates within you a sense of indignation. You believe that you are a victim of injustice and your sense of right cries out for redress and perhaps even revenge.

You wish that the individual who caused you so much pain were here in your presence so that you could punish him. And when you cannot have this satisfaction, you get eaten up inside by your own anger.

It is at this time that you must take control of yourself if you are to come away without too much pain. Any kind of betrayal creates terrible hurt. However, most often, there really isn't much one can do except strike out at the betrayer and try to punish him. If you have rights that have been violated, then, by all means, seek redress. If there has been injustice, then, demand that justice be given to you.

However, if, after doing this, nothing happens and all that is left for you to do is curse, be angry and feel resentment; then, I suggest you try to simply forget your betrayer. Wipe him out of your mind. Since there is a little or nothing that you can do, do not allow him to make your life miserable. Since he does not care at all about you, what you should do is to expend your energies on others more worthy of your love and attention.

Indifference is perhaps the most solid sign of not caring. So much so that in some circles, simply ignoring a person and treating him as though he does not even exist is perhaps the supreme insult. By convincing yourself that he is no longer a priority in your life, you will turn to others more important to you. In so doing, your betrayer will slowly but surely fade away in your mind. Your anger and bitterness will subside. And your frustrations will surely die a slow death.

PARTLY TO BLAME

A LETTER OF A VERY articulate wife of many years and mother of a number of children revealed several dimensions to the problem of marital infidelity.

One of these is the unwillingness of the husband to leave his family and go off with his very young mistress. Perhaps it is because he knows only too well what are the consequences of this kind of relationship. Surely he is aware that his mistress' "love" for him is a love of convenience. It is more of a symbiotic union wherein "I need your body and the sexual pleasure it offers me (husband) and "I want your money and the material benefits you can give me (mistress)" is the name of the game. If there is true, deep and meaningful love between the husband and the mistress; if his wife has repeatedly told him she no longer loves him; if his children resent him and no longer respect him; if his wife keeps asking him to get out; if all this is happening, then why not leave? Perhaps it is because the man knows that his affair is only good enough for an affair and the chances of it evolving into something long-lasting are slim.

I believe very strongly that there are men who simply cannot make up their minds about whether to leave the wife for a mistress or leave the mistress and go back to the wife and family. They prefer having their proverbial cake and eating it too. What usually happens though, is that, in the end, they are left with the worst of two worlds. Their family life is miserable and full of all kinds of conflicts and tensions; so too are their affairs. There is no security, no stability in either. And, instead of making up their minds one way or the other, they insist on playing on both sides of the fence.

If the wife allows this situation to persist, then she is partly to blame. It can go on only if she permits it. I did not say she "wanted" it. I am merely stating that unless she brings the situation to a head, it can go on and on. Then, she will be presented with a condition that is fast normalizing itself and becoming the status quo. What the wife can do is insist on the resolution of the affair. Either the man remains with his mistress and gets out, or he leaves his woman and remains with the family.

Some counselors may disagree with me and plead for patience and prayer. I believe in patience and especially prayer. However, endless patience only encourages the philanderer to carry on "a while longer." And prayer without some movement to help oneself is like asking God to do it all. Prayer asking for wisdom on what to do – Yes! Prayer asking God to do it for you – No!

Unless the woman exercises a measure of control over the situation, the situation will control her. She must be willing to risk losing her man in order to gain a more solid relationship. If she decides to take the road of patience without end, she will most likely end up with an affair without end.

BREAKING POINT IN MARRIAGE

HE WAS A MAN who knew how to hurt. His tongue was sharp, his vocabulary precise. And his words usually found their mark. They hit her right square where it hurts, in the heart. During their exchanges, he almost always got the better of it all. She would back away into her room, lock the door and cry her heart out.

What hurt most was the fact that he never patched her up. He simply left her to bleed all by herself. He never said he was sorry, never apologized, never made the first move to reconcile. It was always up to her to go to him. She did so because, in spite of everything, her love for him had stood strong.

Now that was beginning to change and she feared where it would lead to. She had never entertained thoughts of leaving him before, but now, in the silence of her heart, these thoughts flashed by on occasion.

She was a good woman. Only a good woman could put up with his ways. A woman of lesser patience would have said goodbye long ago. Why she had been able to hang in there all these years was a surprise even to her.

She was an emotionally battered and abused woman. And she had taken it all quietly and without many complaints.

Now she found herself fighting back. She was less apt to make the first move to fix things up. In fact, she realized that now, she was willing to go on for days without reconciliation, whereas before, she would always be in a big rush to right things. Perhaps it was because her love for him was fading. The cooling was not surprising. She had been reaching the breaking point and she was unwilling to go beyond it. Somehow could see no real prospect for change in his ways and she was faced with living with his harshness the rest of her days. For the first time in her married life, she wondered if life without him might not be better, very much better.

We all have breaking point beyond which we refuse to move. We all can take only so much pain. We all have limits to our love. Love is vibrant. It is living. It can be healthy or it may fall prey to sickness and disease. And it may die a swift or a lingering death.

The problem with so many married couples is that they take their love for granted. Like a man who abuses his health, they inflict damage on their relationship.

Please remember that whenever hurt and pain visit a marriage, it scars and marks the relationship. And if the damage is to be contained and kept to a minimum, it must be patched up. People who cannot say "sorry" usually end up losing their beloved. Those who are insensitive that they fail to recognize the need to apologize, find themselves alone and abandoned. More important, we must learn how to avoid hurting the ones we love. Though we may ask for forgiveness and get it, we cannot erase the memory of the pain. This is what may live in long after we have received the assurances that all is well again.

FAILURE IN MARRIAGE

One of the greatest dangers to a successful marriage is one of the spouses' inability or refusal to face a problem which is becoming a serious threat to their relationship. The danger becomes even greater when both of them make a silent contract to ignore some kind of trouble that could weaken and lessen their love for each other.

I am reminded of a pretty wife who refused to face the fact that her husband was playing around with other women. When she got word about his escapades from a number of reliable sources, she confronted her husband. He was quick to deny it all. Instead of pursuing the matter to a more logical conclusion, the wife immediately broke off the discussion.

In spite of repeated warnings by her closest friends, she insisted on dropping the matter then and there.

Well, to make a long story short, she had a rude awakening six months later when the parents of a young girl came to the house and accused the wife's husband of getting their daughter pregnant.

Then the roof caved in on both spouses. What else could you expect when people run away from their problems? They do not realize that sooner or later their problems will catch up with them. Human beings can run fast, but problems have a tremendous staying power if they are not resolved. People run out of breath. Problems don't.

Many of us are like the ostrich that buries its head in the sand whenever it finds itself in danger.

We refuse to face our problems and try to resolve them. Instead, we turn our backs and refuse to look. Some of us even look at the problem straight in the eye and deny its very existence.

It's a little bit like my friend who was scared to death of the dentist. He refused to visit the doctor until it came to a point when they had to extract all of his teeth. Or like another friend of mine who would not be convinced about the wisdom of seeing a doctor about a nagging pain in the stomach. He was afraid of what the findings might be. He thought it might be cancer. He didn't see the doctor in spite of his friends' urgings. Eight months later he died of stomach cancer.

We all have problems. That's life. Nothing unusual about that. Besides, the good Lord gave us brains with which to resolve our problems. We can grow and mature if we learn to cope with our difficulties. We remain children emotionally when we run away from our problems and refuse to even admit that they exist.

Bob Garon

When a man tries walking through life with his eyes closed, you can be sure he is going to get hurt.

WHEN ONCE HAPPY MARRIAGES CRASH DIVE

THE YOUNG WOMAN had met him six months before and it was love at first sight. He was the "tall, dark, and handsome." type of man with a charming personality. He was so "charming" that women would line up in order to fall all over him. And he responded by obliging them. Although he declared his undying love for her, and her alone, he constantly cheated on her.

It wasn't long before she learned about it. She had hoped against hope that their love was so intense that it would serve to keep him faithful to her; that she would be enough to satisfy his needs; that their love would sound the end of his philandering. Now, her mind told her that it just wasn't so. Was it because their love had not grown? As strong as she thought it to be? Or, perhaps she wasn't taking care of him enough? Or, maybe there was something wrong with him, his ability to commit himself to one woman?

In effect, it was some of all these and other factors. What soon become clear to her was that the chances of being faithful to her in marriage were slim indeed. It was pretty much a foregone conclusion that she would have to share her bed with other women. She knew that she would not be able to handle that kind of situation for very long and that she should end the relationship now. However, there was something preventing her from so doing.

Perhaps, it was pride. What would all her friends say? They might see it as a negative reflection on her. Or, maybe it was fear. Fear of not getting another man. Fear that the virginity she lost to him would prove to be an obstacle to an enduring relationship with a potential suitor.

And so, she did not say goodbye. Instead, she stayed with her relationship. Perhaps it was also because she felt that she had given too much of herself to withdraw. Her personal investment was too great, too sizeable, too emotionally intense to simply walk away.

So many men and women do likewise when they get caught in similar circumstances. Instead of cutting their losses and getting out, they hang in there and slip deeper into a situation they *know* and *feel* will not end happily.

Remember that relationships constantly evolve. What was a happy marriage for many years can turn and crash dive. Things can get so bad that the couple is experiencing a real hell. When all else fails and they are faced with the prospect of either bearing it or separating, some choose to go on believing that it is their duty to do the former. Others see it differently. They cut their losses and leave.

When one is faced with a once-upon-a-time beautiful love that has degenerated into something unworkable, one should not feel everything will be lost if he walks away. The happy memories are still there. There were good times and they should not be forgotten. The fact that the dark night has fallen over a relationship should not cause one to deny the beautiful sunny skies of the past. Such a relationship isn't a total loss.

COMPROMISE IN HUMAN RELATIONS

THE ARGUMENT WAS getting more heated by the minute. He was saying that it wasn't so; she, insisting that it was. Married for many years, disagreements were nothing new. However, they had learned how to call it a day when things were beginning to get out of hand.

"Let's not talk about it for a while," she said wearily, "I need space."

He agreed to call off his attack. Both took time to allow things to cool. They became silent and went off in different directions. She did some work in the kitchen; he watched television. Later that evening, the discussion resumed. This time, both were careful not to provoke unduly. Instead, they had a rather calm talk and came to an agreement about the controversy.

It is almost impossible for married couples *not* to have disagreements. They simply live too close to each other. And their everyday dealings give rise to all kinds of possible conflicts. Though they continue to love intensely, the countless opportunities for disagreement are always there. And, unless a couple is able to work out some kind of method of dealing with their differences, arguments will arise and very often get out of control.

One useful way to cope with arguments is to call a moratorium on all discussions for a while. At least, until emotions cool and perspectives clear up enough to enable the couple to resume discussing without raising the chances of an untoward conclusion to their disagreement.

There comes a time in argumentation when neither side seems to be able to communicate what it wants to say very effectively. Then, frustration sets in. And frustration usually leads to anger. And anger provokes more anger. And, when two angry people try to make a point, chances are that the results will *not* be very positive. Most likely, this scenario will end up creating lots of hurt feelings on both sides.

If only the couple can agree on some kind of pre-arranged signal that *both sides* promise to respect *no matter how strongly* they feel. If only they can discipline themselves enough to *temporarily* break off the discussion when the signal is given by either party; then, space will be accorded to both sides. Time is one of the essences in allowing two people to cool off. And, the agreed upon signal does precisely that give time.

Remember that when both partners have cool heads, their chances of coming to an accord which is acceptable to the two of them are infinitely greater. Unless they succeed in accepting some kind of method to give time and space, I predict a lot of unnecessary hurt and inconclusive arguments that will only serve to weaken their relationship.

COURTSHIP DOESN'T END WITH MARRIAGE

MANNY AND ESTER were at it again. Same old argument. Same old conclusion. Same old wound opened again.

Feeling completely frustrated and helpless, Manny retired to his room where he sat on the side of the bed and put his face in his hands.

Ester came in softly, sat down beside him, leaned her head on his shoulder and said, "What has happened to us, Manny? Three years of marriage and we seem to be growing apart from each other."

"Yeah," said Manny, in a whisper. "It isn't like the good old days anymore, is it?"

Too many couples like Manny and Ester look back upon their days of courtship with great longing and, at the same time, with a certain amount of pain. Pain because it hurts to see how far they have regressed in their love for one another. And as the song goes, "Those were days, my friend, we thought would never end." But they have ended.

There is a longing for those days because it was then that each appeared to understand the other. Why did things go so smoothly then? Because they really opened up to each other; because they spent long hours probing each other's mind and heart; because there were no secrets between them; because they were frank and truthful with each other.

Things were wonderful then because there was the thrill and excitement of discovery. To look into the deepest recess of a loved one's heart is just about the most memorable adventure in a person's life. With every date came new discoveries, new realization. Every intense conversation revealed hidden beauties never before suspected. This expectation, this "what-will-I-find-next" attitude made courtship all so exciting. Piecing together the personality and the heart of the loved one was such an enjoyable challenge. Most of all, it was the exhilarating sense of security one felt in knowing that here, among the millions of people the world over, "is a man I understand and who reads me like an open book. (And who loves me dearly in spite of my stupidity.)"

If countless people down through the years have been inspired by the touching romance of a Romeo and Juliet, it is because there is in all of us that overwhelming desire to reach out to another person and to know him truly and authentically. There is in all of us the corresponding longing to be reached in the same sincere way. However, this is such a rare happening that when we see it portrayed on the silver screen, we all identify with Romeo and Juliet.

If so many couples are unhappy and disillusioned after a few years of marriage, it is because they do not realize that courtship does not end with marriage. On the contrary, courtship is supposed to shift into high gear after the wedding.

If so many husbands and wives are bored with one another it is because, like an overconfident basketball team, they have relaxed their play. With this letup in effort, they have soon found themselves disoriented, confused, demoralized and far behind.

If there are so many unhappy marriages, it is because couples have forgotten the very great difference between courtship and marriage. Courtship is a couple-of-days-a-week- affair. Marriage is a twenty-four-hour-a-day courtship.

FORMULA FOR A MARITAL DISASTER

Situation: A married woman has felt only neglect from her husband over the years. He has not attended to her needs in spite of her devotion to him. He has distanced himself from her. And, finally, all the indications point to his having an affair with another woman.

During all these years, her love and respect for him have been slowly dying. Then, one day, she finds herself irresistibly drawn to another man. At first, she does not take it very seriously. However, after some time, she consents to sleeping with him. Soon, she finds herself in a full-blown affair and isn't quite sure how she got there. Her head is full of all kinds of contradictions. Her heart is pulling one way and her head another. Her husband is unaware of what's happening.

She wrote me a long letter. Too long to publish verbatim. I have decided to extract some lines and comment on them. Others, I am sure, are in similar situations.

"What is happening to me is serious and embarrassing. I'm afraid. What if my husband finds out, I'll lose everything. But for sure, deep in my heart, I have no regrets of loving him (the lover) and having an affair with him."

You have no regrets because you no longer love your husband. You do not care about hurting him anymore. What you are afraid of is losing the material comfort you have gained through your married years. And, you are worried about what your friends and family will say *when* they find out. I said *when* because it is only a question of time until they learn the truth. There is no way you can keep this a secret indefinitely. One day, you or he will make a slip and your husband or a friend will know. Then, the whole story will begin to come to light, piece by piece. And there will be little you can do to stop it. It is the way it always happens.

"On the eve of my wedding anniversary, we had another intimate moment. After the act, he told me to forget him and go back to my husband. He said he pities me because I am devoting so much time to him. He said he realizes that this is not good for me."

It is significant that he told you this after the act. I wonder if he isn't fooling you. Of course, he enjoys taking you to bed. Besides, you are wealthy compared to him. That worries me. I do not believe he is deeply convinced when he tells you to go back to your husband. I believe he wants the affair to continue.

"I am a decent woman, a good mother. Can you believe me?"

Yes, I can and do believe you. Decent women get fed up and fall out of love. Decent women still have needs that are crying to be filled. Decent women get lonely and are vulnerable. Decent women, good mothers, get themselves into affairs. You are troubled, worried. You are full of guilt feelings. You are looking for some kind of solution. That is why you are writing to me. If you were not bothered emotionally and morally, you would not need to write.

"After he told me I should go back to my husband, I cried hard. I was not prepared for his words. I didn't expect them so soon. I knew that someday it would be parting time, but not that soon… Maybe he was touched by my tears. He said to just forget what he said. He also cried… So I gave him another chance."

A chance for what? To continue a confused relationship? The two of you, it seems to me, cannot make up your minds. Your affair in its present state cannot go on forever. Something is going to have to give somewhere, someday. And I think that someday will be soon. There seems to be no direction. The two of you are going around in circles, all the while getting in deeper. You are losing control of the events instead of controlling them. And this kind of situation is a sure formula for disaster.

PLAYING WITH FIRE

"MY HUSBAND IS beginning to suspect something, I think. He hints about it by telling me stories about other people. However, I know him well and I can sense that he suspects me. He isn't angry though. Maybe it is because he no longer loves me and is having an affair of his own."

You may be right. Perhaps he does suspect. Spouses, even when they no longer love each other, have strong and oftentimes accurate feelings about these things. If he no longer loves you and is himself having an affair, then it may very well be that he is hoping that you are in love with some man, then each of you can go his/her separate way.

"My lover's desire for me is more intense now. However, I don't want to have sex with him anymore. It's too much, and besides, it's wrong. I am certain that I can still love him without physical and sexual attachment I want to stop the sex, but I don't want to stop loving him. We can still be lovers, but without sex."

Come now. Let's be practical. You are having a full-blown affair with a man you obviously love very much.

You have been having sex regularly with him. And now, suddenly, you intend to carry on as before, but minus the sex? You must be joking. Surely you are not serious about those words.

You have allowed this affair to go "all the way." The barriers that lead to sexual intercourse have been destroyed already. You cannot be expected to rebuild them because it is impossible to do so. Continue your affair and stay out of bed? The odds against that happening are overwhelming. The only way to stay out of bed is to get out of his life. Forget the Platonic love. It won't work. Have him or don't have him. But don't half have him.

"I want to try to control myself and be a good mother again. I cannot tell you that I will be a good wife again because my love for him has already died."

You are playing with fire. And as sure as you are reading these lines you *will* get burned. This is not a healthy relationship that you are having with your lover. Too many complications. Too much confusion. Too many uncertainties and unknown. Too much stress and tension. In short, too many odds against it working out.

Most of all, it isn't honest. All this drama and behind - the - back type of affair is just not healthy. Go back to your husband and clear the air. Don't love him? Tell him! Feel he doesn't love you? Tell Him! Think he's having an affair? Tell him! Want to separate? Tell him! See what happens.

Get things clear with your marriage first. Events are out of control at this time. Get a grip on them. Also, get help! See a good counselor who can work through your complex problems with you one at a time.

While you are doing all this, don't forget the one upstairs. You need His help. Ask for it. You are terribly confused. He can help you clear up your confusion. He's free, loving and always there.

WHEN THE MOTHER-IN-LAW DESTROYS MARRIAGE

MUCH HAS BEEN SAID and written about mothers-in-law. The truth of the matter is that most of them are positive forces in the lives of a young couple. They try to help as best they can and care enough to allow the young couple to do their own thing by standing clear and letting them live out their own lives.

However, there are those who either are unaware of the damage they are causing or are so fixated on their own desperate needs and simply get so involved in a newly married couple's existence that they cause unbelievable hurt. And, if nothing is done to curb their influence, they often go on and cause the destruction of a marriage. There are mothers-in-law who cannot seem to outgrow the mothering phase of their lives. They cannot seem to switch gears and become that much needed friend of their sons or daughters. Instead, they intrude (often rudely) into the affairs of the new couple. They make decisions in the new household that are clearly not theirs to make. They put heavy and undue pressure on the son or daughter and his/her spouse. They dominate and push the couple around.

The mother-in-law who does this may think she is winning. And she *does* win many battles, but, in the end, she almost always loses the war. And in the process, more often than not, she loses her child.

And what about the poor couple that is the victim of a tyrannical mother-in-law? What happens to the two youngsters who are trying to make a go of their marriage under such trying circumstances? If the man is a Mama's Boy or the girl is a Mama's Girl, then the marriage is almost always doomed to fail. This is so because the Mama's Boy does not really want to live independently from his mother. He actually likes having Mama decide from him and run his life. He is so used to having her run his life that he feels secure about allowing her to continue doing so for the rest of his days. Of course, the woman who has married such a man quickly experiences a rude awakening. She finds herself competing with her mother-in-law. It is an uneven battle. The mother-in-law is too solidly entrenched to be defeated. She knows her son only too well. She is aware of his weakness vis-à-vis her and she is quick to exploit them. Her daughter-in-law does not stand a chance in a toe-to-toe fight.

All the little one can do is try to rescue her husband and get him as far away as possible from his mother. No matter if she suffers financially and materially. If she is to save her marriage, she *must at all costs* get away. The sooner the better.

Her husband must grow independent of his mother. She must find a way to move him out of the circle of her influence. If she cannot succeed in doing this, then, I believe there is little chance of happiness. The mother-in-law will surely not change. Unless the wife is willing to adapt to the ways of her in-laws, she needs to break away with her husband. Because under his mother's immediate influence, he will never really change substantially; it is pure fantasy to think the couple can work something out without going off on their own.

LAWS IN FAVOR OF MEN

I ONCE PUBLISHED a letter from an angry married woman. She was commenting on how unfair an extramarital affair can be for the wife and family. She insisted that since the country is without divorce laws, there should be stricter laws to protect the wife from the "claim" of the mistress. She asked that the penalties for erring husbands be increased and strictly implemented.

She has many valid points. The fact that there are no divorce laws in the country allows the man to be bolder in his affairs. Of course, she can always file a case against him for adultery and concubinage. However, how often do these cases amount to anything? The courts tend to use the conciliatory and appeasement approaches. They try so hard to avoid any kind of breakup that, in the end, the woman who wants to end it all and get some kind of material protection finally gives up in utter frustration.

She may ask him to leave the house. If he refuses, she can do nothing. If she walks out in protest, it is "abandonment." If she separates, she almost never gets anything near the kind of material support she deserves. And, more often than not, she ends up with absolutely nothing and is forced to fend for herself. She is then in the sometimes desperate position of having to support her children while he goes off to start a new life with the other woman.

Let's face it. The laws are loaded in favor of the men. If divorce were allowed (and I am not saying it should) I believe men would not be so brazen about their affairs. If the wife could divorce him and get just about everything he has, husbands would be more careful about getting involved. When my kid divorced his wife, who was an alcoholic, he lost the house, the car, his bank account, everything except his clothes. And most of his salary ended up in her pocket. And if he does not abide by the conditions of support, he runs the risk of going to jail. His wife may suffer emotionally, but at least her financial needs are met.

It is true that most men get away with their affairs. The price they have to pay is relatively light. If only they got hit hard; if only the consequences of their wanderings caused them pain; if they were made to truly own up to their financial responsibilities to the family; then I believe they would think more before jumping into bed with the other woman.

It is difficult for a wife to witness her man running off and sharing with another woman the fruits of their (hers and his, not the mistress) labor. She feels it is some kind of ugly fraud, another form of stealing. And she has a point. Why should he be allowed to unilaterally share their hard-earned material wealth with a woman who has absolutely no right to it? Why should he get away with spending on his mistress her inheritance and that of the children? And even if the husband insists that his family does not go without anything, his argument holds no water. It is not a matter of justice that we are talking about.

I agree that women do not have enough legal protection from their philandering husbands. I agree that the implementation of the laws (weak though they may be) is loose. I think that other alternatives should be given. If divorce is unacceptable, then something should be done to make the spouse having the affair pay a price that is commensurate with the damage and pain he has caused. Until this happens, men will continue fooling around and not worry much about the consequences. Right now, there is little to deter men who wish to wander off. Until there is, they will continue to wander, and wander and…

UNHAPPY SPOUSE

I REMEMBER TALKING to a former beauty queen some years ago. She was a very happily married woman whose deep love for her husband was evident for all to see. We were having dinner in a friend's home and there was a big crowd of people present. A man came by, sat at the table and, after a while, started making passes at her. She seemed not to mind him and soon the man went away to try his luck somewhere else. I asked her how she felt about what had just happened.

"What happened?" she asked, visibly surprised at my question.

"Didn't you notice that he was making passes at you?" I asked.

"He sure was. Didn't you notice?"

"No, I didn't."

And I believe she really did not notice what was very obvious to me. We talked about it and she told me that she hardly noticed if men made passes at her. I explained to her that it was so because of her deep love and meaningful marriage. I told her things would surely change the moment her marriage went into a dive and she found herself unhappy with her relationship. She merely smiled and remained silent.

A couple of years later, I ran into her again and was surprised to learn that she had separated from her husband and was now living with another man. I asked her what happened.

"You were right. When I caught him fooling around, I was so disillusioned, so hurt. My love for him died. Then I started noticing men noticing me. And I said to myself: 'If he cannot respect me and love me, then, there are others who will.' There were. I decided to leave him."

I believe there is an axiom in love that holds true in all love relationships. It is this: "the intensity of the temptation to have an affair is directly proportional to the level of unhappiness in a marriage. I do *not* believe that the same temptation strikes everyone with the same intensity. Take three women caught up in the same circumstances. Two are very happily married. The third is miserable. The same temptation may not at all affect the happy ones while the third is greatly disturbed.

An unhappy spouse is a good setup for an affair. The happy, contented spouse is relatively "temptation-free" because he/she is not bothered, is not looking elsewhere for the fulfillment of needs. If a man feels that his various needs are taken care of, then the chances of his falling are slimmer even if they are still present. Why? Because he feels that he has a lot to lose. On the other hand, the man who is totally unfulfilled has little to lose by risking an affair. In fact, if he gives in to the temptation, it is because he perceives that some personal "good" will come of it.

It is important to understand this if one intends to guard his marriage. The signs will be clear. Unhappiness, a lack of fulfillment, felt needs that remain unattended to: all these things increase the chances of an affair developing. There is no doubt about it.

BETRAYING TRUST

THE WIFE WAS FURIOUS when she found out. He had promised her that he would never again see the mistress he had left six months before. Now, he got caught in a lie. He had said he would be out of town when. in fact. he never left the city. Trouble is that he was seen with her in the car and the sighting was reported to his wife.

That was when all hell broke loose. At first, she was angry and spoke harsh words. Then, she wept and pleaded. Then, she got angry again and screamed and threatened to leave him. The children were upset and gave him the cold shoulder.

He tried to explain that he only saw her because she was in trouble, needed his help, and he pitied her. His wife sneered at him, and the children looked silently unbelieving. He gave up trying to explain and settled down for a long siege.

And well he might. It is not surprising that nobody believes his story. Neither do I for that matter. Neither would a thousand onlookers. It is the kind of fairy tale that only the most naive would lend any credence to. I would rather think that he longed for the "good old day" when the affair was going on full-blast and he was enjoying himself considerably. I think the mistress was not in such distress as he would want us to believe. Rather. It was a "let's-get-in-touch-again" type of meeting. The wife was quite justified in flying off the handle--although I do not see how that outburst did anything at all to strengthen their love or what's left of it.

His story is not believable because his leaving the mistress in the first place was not what you would call "voluntary." In fact, he did so very reluctantly indeed, and only after terrific pressure from all sides. So, any kind of meeting with the woman he so enjoyed would have to be suspect.

The result of all this, of course, is another monumental setback in the relationship. One would have to suspect that there is absolutely no love left in his marriage and that he left the mistress and reconciled with his wife only as a matter of convenience.

When a man discovered having an affair and agrees to break it up and comes home, he should know that his marriage has suffered a terrible blow that could, in effect, signal the end to it all in spite of the reconciliation. He should understand that his wife's level of trust in him is down to zero and that the burden of responsibility for rebuilding that trust lies squarely on him. Consequently, he will be watched and watched carefully. That is the price he must pay for his indiscretions. And *any* kind of contract whatsoever with the mistress will mark the return to square one. *Any kind*! No matter what the reason, if he values his marriage at all, he *must* stay away from the former mistress. This is essential if the reconciliation is to hold. If the mistress needs help, he should be the last person to volunteer any kind of aid.

CHALLENGES IN MARRIAGE

HE WAS INTELLIGENT, talented, but more on the quiet side. Conscientious and hard-working, he was known by his friends to be a very good father and a loyal husband. For these reasons, everyone was surprised when they learned that he had a young mistress. He seemed the least likely to fool around with another woman.

Part of the answer (only a part) lay in the character and personality of his wife. A fine woman with an unusual level of talent, she was a very aggressive person in every area of her life. She excelled in business. One reason was her strong personality. A leader and an organizer, she got things done quickly and efficiently. She ran her house as family and as well as her business.

If she was such a super person, then why would that be a cause for trouble? He should have been happy that he had such a woman as his wife. He should have, but he wasn't.

Success can also be a liability in some circumstances. Just as it isn't easy to live with a saintly person, neither is it that simple to be married to a smashing success. Especially when you feel you are being eclipsed by your wife. When everyone is talking about her; then you need to be a very special kind of man to be able to handle that kind of situation. It's a little bit like being married to Margaret Thatcher.

No doubt there are men who do not mind their wives outdistancing them in their careers. But these men have some special traits that allow them to feel comfortable with the situation. They are self-assured and not easily threatened by all the success of their women. Perhaps it is because they feel they have had their own share of success and are happy to see their wives enjoying the excitement of succeeding and being recognized. Or maybe it is because they have no aspirations of succeeding so much themselves. Finally, there are those who prefer to ride on the success of others rather than forge ahead and make their own mark.

Clearly, the husband at the beginning of this column was not at ease with being a "second placer" in the family. He was too embarrassed or proud to open up his feelings to his wife, however, and he suffered in silence. He felt as though he was always running hard to stay even a distant second to his wife.

Deep down inside, he longed to assume that role of leader and protector in a relationship. In his house, his wife was the undisputed leader who was surely in no need of protection.

It should come as no surprise then that when he fell in love with another woman, she was the gentle and shy type of person who looked up to him for both leadership and protection. And he relished his new role. Somehow, it made him "feel like a man again."

The moral of this story is that the alternative, dynamic and successful career woman is *not* for just any man. Whoever gets involved with her must surely be able to handle the challenges that she brings to the relationship.

TOTAL FORGIVENESS...?

HE WAS IN LOVE with his wife. He never doubted it. However, he had gone out of town on a business trip and hotel rooms can be very lonely places. And when she sat in the lobby sending him signals that she was available, he succumbed to the temptation. He did not love her. She was young, well-built and the sexual drive within him was swiftly aroused.

The affair did not last long. One night. When he returned to the city, it was all over. All over. All over, in a way. The memory of what happened lingered. So did the strong guilt feelings. Months later, he was still bothered by the brief fling. He never opened it up to his wife. He reasoned that she would be so terribly hurt that their relationship would be dealt a heavy blow. And perhaps she would never forgive him. Even if she did, she would not forget. Not ever. And the memory of his infidelity would haunt him forever. So he decided to keep it all to himself.

However, even if she did not know and he went about doing things as though nothing had happened, he continued to be troubled. Maybe it was because he was a decent man with a conscience. The guilt was exacting a heavy price in emotional tension. When his beloved wife was kind to him, when she showed him affection, when she paid no attention to the passes of other men, when she made love to him, then the feelings of guilt intensified. If only she fooled around, even once, then that would even things up. It was difficult living with such a good and faithful woman when he had been such a double-crosser.

Pretending was the most stressful part of living with her. He felt that he was something like Dr. Jekyll and Mr. Hyde. He kept wondering if she would still love him should she learn about his infidelity. And, what would his teenage children say and think?

When a man, a decent man, has a casual affair, it seems to me that he must pay an exorbitant price for his pleasure. The aftermath of the sexual involvement is by far more costly than the monetary rewards he gives the woman.

Of course, if he is a man who isn't very bothered by infidelity, he may be able to handle the tension a lot better. He will rationalize it away. He will tell himself that man is basically polygamous (highly debatable), that everybody is doing it (not true), that what his wife does not know won't hurt her (ha!ha!).

If he is a man who has no conscience at all when it comes to extra-marital affairs, there will be little or no guilt at all. Having different women in his bed is no more serious than changing his socks.

The intensity of the guilt feeling will be determined by the extent that his conscience and values place a premium on fidelity, loyalty, marital honesty and religious convictions. The less there is of this, the more freedom he will have to feel around and not have to feel guilty about it.

FORGETFUL HUSBANDS

PERHAPS THE MOST COMMON suffering of women who have been married more than five years is the feeling of not being loved as much as before. I said "feeling." Maybe they are loved even more than before. Yet they "feel" they are not.

Perhaps it is because they feel neglected and unappreciated. The husband no longer kisses her as often as he used to. He doesn't hug her as much and with as much affection (I didn't say *passion*) as in the "old days."

He used to compliment her on the way she dressed, her hairdo, and her superb cooking. Now, he seems to take it all for granted. She wonders if he even notices.

Let's face it! It is difficult for us to be consistent over a long period of time. We get sloppy and tend to forget and neglect "little" things. And husbands are among the most notorious offenders. They forget to kiss their wives. They neglect to comment on many of those little things that are so important to them. They are either unaware or insensitive, or both.

If you think that you are one of those wives who feels neglected and taken for granted, perhaps you should cut out this column and place it somewhere where he is sure to see it.

Below is a piece that puts the message across in an unmistakable way:

Amid the cares of married Strife,
In spite of toil and business life,
If you value your wife
Tell her so!

When days are dark and deeply blue
She has her troubles, same as you.
Show her that your love is true —
Tell her so!

There was a time a time you thought is bliss
To get the favor of one kiss;
A dozen now won't come amiss—
Tell her so!

Don't act, if she has passed per prime
As tho' to please her were a crime;
If ever You loved her, now's the time —
Tell her so!

She'll return, for each caress,
A hundredfold of tenderness!
Hearts like hers made to bless!
Tell her so.

Bob Garon

You are hers and hers alone;
Well you know she's all your own;
Don't wait to carve it on a stone —
Tell her so.

FALLING IN LOVE WITH AN IMAGE

WHEN HE MARRIED her, he loved her deeply. It was as if she was all that he had imagined a woman to be. She sported good looks, a sparkling personality, and a great deal of talent. She loved him dearly. At first, he believed that their marriage was a perfect relationship, an ideal love.

With the passing of time, however, his thinking changed. Instead, he began to see a number of flaws in the fiber that made up their love. There were conflicts now where there were none before. There was argumentation where before, there was peace. There arose discord where before there was only harmony.

He began to think that the woman he now saw was not the person he married. In fact, he wondered how he could have been so mistaken in the first place. How could he have missed what was so obvious to him now?

How? It was easy. When we fall in love, we most often have in mind the kind of woman we would like to have. Usually, she is the type whom we feel could answer our needs. The problem lies in the fact that we oftentimes bend the reality that is the person to fit into the mold that we have fashioned for her. In other words, we have created in our minds an image of the woman of our dreams. We are in love with that image. We nurture it in our heads and in our hearts, we long for it to become a reality. The danger lies in our failure to distinguish the real from the imagined.

I remember a young man madly in love with a woman whose character and personality was a perfect formula for trouble. Although everyone saw the situation quite clearly and warned him about it. He was not listening. Instead, he pursued his relationship. After some time and many conflicts, the reality of the situation began to emerge. He realized that she was not the woman for him and broke off with her. Actually, the girl had not changed. The woman he said goodbye to was the same woman he had first fallen in love with. He had, in fact, only seen her as she truly was towards the end of their relationship. In the beginning, he was in love with what he thought she was, the image he had constructed in his mind.

We have to be careful of the images we build. When we look at people, we need to be aware of what is truly them and not what comes from the working of our own minds. We must be sensitive enough to be able to tell the difference between what is the image we have built and what is the true essence of the character and personality before us.

Falling in love with an image can be disastrous. If we expect the person we love to take on the likeness of the image we finalized about, the consequence will be painful for all concerned. Reality has a way of striking back at those who play with it. Taking a realistic view of a person and then accepting what we see is the beginning of deep and *true* love.

A COMPLICATED SITUATION

When a man has an affair and found out, the discovery creates a great upheaval that can mark those involved for many years and often for life. Most affairs get to be very complicated. There are so many dimensions that have to be taken into consideration that rarely are affairs simple.

There are, however, some affairs that are especially complex. Take this one, for example.

A husband has a mistress. The wife finds out. Lots of trouble follows. He continues the affair in spite of the tension it produces in the family. The wife gets sick and, after a while, she dies.

The way is now clear for the man to change the status of the affair to one of legitimate courtship. His children, though, have some thoughts of their own about the matter.

They blame their father for what happened. They brand him as the killer of the woman they loved so deeply. They see him as the betrayer, the disloyal husband who drove their mother to her grave. They believe he has cheated their Mom, and they resent him for it. Now that their Mom is "out of the way," they assume that Dad and his mistress are "having a celebration." The pressure is off the two of them. So children decide to apply some of their own pressures on them.

They refuse to accept her as their stepmother. Although Dad is trying his best to influence kids to accept her, they don't. This angers him. His temper flares. The children react by going to their rooms and giving him the silent treatment. Before long, there is a continuous state of siege in the house. They fear him. They hate him… and the woman he loves. They cannot wait to grow old enough to leave home and support themselves.

At the same time, they feel guilty. Guilty because they are fighting their Dad. Guilty because they are not fighting hard enough for the "honor" of their deceased mother. Guilty because they feel that the love and attention their father is lavishing on the "other woman" is not rightfully theirs.

The end result of this complicated situation is continuous stress and tension that slowly cause hatred to get the upper hand everywhere.

In such a situation, you can expect everything to go from bad to worse. The Dad is looking after his own needs. The mistress, hers. The children, theirs. It is only Mother who lies peacefully in her grave.

This kind of complicated affair causes so much damage that is takes a lot of doing to even minimize the destruction. Unless the kids and the father get some real help in coping with these exceedingly difficult circumstances, you can be sure that the trail of broken hearts will be long. The hurt that such an affair engenders will last long after the dust settles and the conflict is seemingly over. Psychological wounds as deep as these do not heal very well.

WHEN MARITAL DREAMS ARE QUASHED

WHENEVER PEOPLE CRACK jokes about marriage, it oftentimes has to do with "loss of freedom." There is something about commitment to a person that destroys a number of options that we would otherwise have. There is a mark of exclusivity in marriage that closes off some avenues to a spouse.

Getting "involved" with someone else is not allowed. There is a kind of finality about the marital commitment. If you miss your spouse; if you are not happy; if you run into someone more desirable; then, you can consider yourself "stuck." There is no way out unless you violate your commitment. Because the marital promise does not allow room for repeal or recall, there is a kind of period that is placed at the end of the sentence. Perhaps this is why so many poke fun at the institution of marriage. There are regrets.

And these regrets are alluded to indirectly in the form of jokes. The man who wishes that he could turn back the hands of time and "unmarry" his wife is full of regrets. Perhaps it is because there is heavy conflict and unbearable pressure between them. Or maybe it is because he is bored and has suddenly met a woman who excites him. Or it might be that his wife is simply no longer attractive to him sexually, emotionally and/or intellectually and he longs for a change.

In this case, the commitment he made is now getting in his way. Especially if he is an honorable man who lives by a strict code of ethics. He does not want to break his commitment. Yet, to allow the status quo to persist is to resign himself to a life that is less than appealing and, in some cases, downright miserable.

The wife who has been abused and feels that his love for her is dying, if not dead; whose former, dreams of marital bliss have been dashed to the ground long ago; whose prospects of future happiness have been dimmed by incessant conflict; this woman also wonders about the commitment she made that fateful day in front of the altar of God. It is difficult for her *not* to have regrets. Especially when she puts aside her children as a factor in the equation. If it were not for them, I believe that countless women would have long ago made a dash for the door.

When dreams are quashed, when reality cuts down former expectations, when needs (some of them basic) remain unfulfilled; then it becomes difficult for a married person *not* to have regrets. It is hard for him *not* to feel that he made a terrible mistake by having committed himself. It is almost inevitable that a certain amount of cynicism about marriage as an institution makes its appearance. This is so because there is a feeling of having been cheated. A sense of having done something stupid.

More than anything, there is a feeling of dread at being caught up in a no-win situation. Hold to one's commitment and suffer indefinitely. Violate one's promise and pay a heavy price. Some make up their minds and move in one direction or another. Some stand still. They think of moving, but never do. They go on, trapped and poking fun as a release for their frustrations.

LOSING A HUSBAND?

SHE DEEPLY LOVED her husband. She would not want to live with any other man. That is why even she could not understand why she got involved with that other man. To be sure, she never loved him. And when it ended, the only regret she had was that it ever took place. When they parted ways, neither of them seemed to feel bad. In fact, both seemed to breathe a sigh of relief that it was over.

How it all started, she could not be sure. Her husband had left town for more than a month. Perhaps she felt lonely. Or maybe bored with the sameness of her days. Anyway, it happened.

Now that it was over, she felt guilt. She believed that what she did was wrong. She felt sorry it ever happened and worried that her marriage would be devastated if her husband ever found out. He was not the type of man to forgive and forget such a thing. If he ever learned about the affair, there was a good chance that their marriage would not survive. And, if it did, surely that damage would be so extensive that the effects of her affair would be deeply felt for years to come. There were few secrets between them. At least on her part. She had never withheld anything from him. But then, she had never had an affair either. It had always been easy to open up to him because there was really nothing much to be ashamed of, nothing that might compromise their marriage.

There were a few times in the past when she had suspected him of having brief flings. However, she was never able to prove anything to substantiate her doubts. He had always denied everything. And now, she was in the same boat.

She had no intention of telling him anything. And, if ever he would question her, she would strongly deny any wrongdoing. She hated the prospect of lying to him. However, she worried even more about her marriage. She had to decide between openness and the sure crisis her frankness would create. She had to make up her mind between getting it all off her chest and striking perhaps a mortal blow to her union, or keeping it to herself and having to carry her burden silently for the rest of her life. She decided to live with her secret. It would be difficult, but better than losing her husband.

It would be difficult to argue with this woman. Only she is the final judge of the ability or inability of her husband to handle such a revelation. Just as parents keep some things away from the children because telling the truth would deeply trouble them, so too is it sometimes necessary for a spouse to withholding information when in her judgment such revelations will do more harm than good.

The problem with this choice of options is the burden that one must carry all alone. Sharing always makes things easier, especially when we can share with our beloved. Having to keep things to oneself is painful, yet when the alternative is the possible destruction of one's relationship, then there is hardly any choice at all.

HOLY WEDLOCK BECOMES "HOLY DEADLOCK"

OFTEN, I HAVE BEEN accused of contributing to the breakup of families. By encouraging spouses of unhappy unions to say goodbye and try to rebuild their lives, critics have leveled a finger at me and said that I have caused marriages to disintegrate.

The fact is that I never *tell* anyone what to do. I am a counsellor. I counsel. I do *not* decide. I discuss options and ask the counselee what he thinks of his choices and their consequences. I ask him to think things over carefully before deciding. And if he chooses *not* to choose, then that is fine by me. My job is to help him, not to do it (whatever *it* may be) for him.

I myself am not liberal when it comes to my marriage. In fact, I am strongly old-fashioned. Through all our years of marriage, Emmy and I have been away from each other exactly *one night.* We lead exciting and meaningful lives. Our work takes us all over the country. However, we have worked hard to make our marriage our top priority in *fact* as well as in words.

I do not believe husbands should fool around. I think even "one-night stands" are detrimental to a healthy marriage. I am still a strong subscriber to the values I preached as a priest. However, I have a problem when it comes to marriages that are devoid of love. I wonder about spouses living together, all the while hating each other. I can understand what it means to make a commitment to each other: however, I also wonder what it all means when one party breaks his promises and makes a mockery of his commitment. I am not sure that the aggrieved one has an obligation to go on upholding her part of the bargain. It seems to me that a marriage contract is between *two* people who make mutual commitment. These promises I think are constitutional. Any contract is.

I promise to pay you for some goods IF you can deliver on this date. If you fail to do so, then, my obligation ceases because you have failed to keep your part of the bargain. In marriage, we promised each other many things. If I break these promises and betray you, are you still bound to swear loyalty and fidelity to me all the while? If so, I am uncomfortable about it. Uncomfortable because it does not seem right and just.

When a marriage is out of control; when love is non-existent; when it is full of anger and bitterness; when betrayal and infidelity is a daily happening; then, I think that holy wedlock has become, as one sociologist termed it, "holy deadlock."

When things have come to this, then it is perhaps time to think of a change.

The alternative is to resign oneself to the status quo. And I do not believe that God put us on this earth to suffer a long life of misery and torment. If things have come to the point where contracts have been broken, commitments betrayed, and love killed, then the rationale of marriage is no longer?

ON TYING THE KNOT

WHEN TWO PEOPLE are madly in love and want to marry, dissuading them from tying the knot can be a more monumental task than conquering Mt. Everest. In the many years that I have spent counselling couples, I have slowly and painfully learned not to get in the way of individuals who tell me they want to contract marriage. Even when a couple comes to me to ask what I think of their relationship, I have understood that what they really want is for me to tell them that all's well and they are sure to be happy ever after.

As I pause and try to remember the counselling I have done in the past, I cannot remember ever being able to convince two people bent on marrying to call the whole thing off. Not even once.

Yet, I can recall many marriages that I was sure would become total disasters. I remember warming couples of the slim chances of success if they went forward. All of them went ahead anyway. An overwhelming majority of those clear-cut cases ended up shattered on the rocks. When parents ask me to try to convince two youngsters not to marry, I refuse because I know that my chances of so doing are just about nil. The only way of stopping them is to separate them. Although this is far from the ideal responses, it stands a better chance of success than trying logic and persuasion.

The fact is that when two people decide that they will marry, they want intellectual and emotional support for that decision. They want confirmation from other quarters. This approval gives them courage to go ahead. It also helps them to overcome the doubts and the intellectual and emotional barriers that cause them to hesitate.

This is so not just when it concerns marriage. Any kind of decision making will cause people to consult others in order to gain approval. Problem is that most of us who decide on something do not want to hear negative responses. So, we do our best to seek out those whom we feel, deep in our hearts, would support our point of view. We consciously or unconsciously avoid those whom we feel would give us feedback that would give us feedback that would dissuade us. Few among us have the kind of strength and courage it takes to knowingly go running to someone who holds a contrary view, just to see if our decision can stand up under the fire of his criticism. We sense that this could (and most likely *would*) weaken our will to go ahead. So, we run to those whom we are reasonably sure will stand by us and give us the approval we seek.

So, the next time someone seeks your opinion or advice about a decision he has already made, spend a few minutes asking him if he has definitely decided to go ahead. If he says "yes" (or he says "no" he hasn't yet decided, but you strongly suspect he has), then you can go ahead and give your advice. However, know that the chances of his following your advice if it contradicts his stated purposes are almost zero. Understand also that should you agree with him, you will indeed have a very happy individual.

I feel good whenever my own sincere beliefs happen to support a friend's decision. Then, all is easy. If, however, my convictions run in the opposite direction, I feel uncomfortable because I know that I cannot in conscience support his decision. That is the price I must pay for remaining true to myself and to my friend.

MARRIAGE BREAK-UP DUE TO SILENCE

HE IS A CUTE little boy. Barely 2 years old. Totally unaware of the disaster that has struck the marriage of his parents. What he does not know is that the absence of his father these past days is the beginning of the end of a marriage that should have never been in the first place.

She is a very good woman, but the extremely quiet type. I said "extremely" quiet, because she rarely speaks, even to her child. It isn't that she is angry or anything of the sort. It is just that she simply has nothing to say. She is living proof that a person can go about her business the whole day and not say a word.

This silence was what was slowly killing him. At first, he could handle it. Then, as the months passed, he became irritated. He would ask her questions and get one-lines for answers. And, if he did not ask, she would remain quiet. It was an extreme case of lack of communication. And it was slowly destroying their relationship, which was never strong to begin with. How could it? They had a whirlwind courtship. In fact, he first dated her when his friends dared him to do so. He won the bet, but soon found everyone expecting them to marry. And since he had never given marriage a serious thought, when her parents asked when they would marry, he gave them a date. And that was all there was to it. They married and the child followed quickly.

Friends who knew them had their doubts about the whole thing. My wife Emmy and I raised the red warning flag. We told them that marriage was a lot more complex than they thought and that they should wait a while. Get to know each other more.

All the advice and warnings went unheeded. They usually do. When two people want to marry, they can hardly ever be dissuaded by logic. And now that it was breaking up, of what use would it be to say to them: I told you so, but you didn't want to listen. All we could do was sit back and watch the disaster happen. We would feel sorry for her because it wasn't anything she did that caused the breakup. It was because she never said anything that it was coming to an end. She never fought or argued. Her husband would have welcomed that. She was a pretty woman, but one quickly tires of a mannequin which cannot talk.

He tried to help her communicate, but it was impossible for her to change. Faced with a lifetime of the same, he gave up and walked away. Sad, but a reality we need to acknowledge.

Until couples understand that marriage is no child's play; that it is deadly serious business for mature adults only; that the consequences of marital failure can cause deep wounds from which recovery will be very difficult; that marital bliss is not assured by a walk down the aisle; until these are not realized, marriages will continue to break up at an alarming rate.

SHARING PROBLEMS WITH ONE'S SPOUSE

He had not been feeling well emotionally lately. The worry and anxiety of a number of problems were weighing heavily on him. He felt himself sliding into depression. His wife sensed something was wrong and repeatedly asked him what it was. He always answered that everything was fine and that she was merely imagining things. In fact, he wanted to share with her his feelings. There was a strong desire to unburden himself, so heavy was his sadness and feeling of alienation.

The reason for holding back was stronger than his desire to share. Because his wife was the type of woman who easily panicked, he was hesitant. Besides, she was a worse worrier than he and had a tendency to exaggerate problems. He felt he had enough of his own troubles without adding to the worries that she would surely experience if he opened up to her. The price he would surely experience if he opened up to her. The price he would have to pay for the comfort of sharing was too high. He decided to keep things to himself and to continue to tell her that "everything was fine."

*****

Vic was in practically the same situation. A wave of sadness had broken over him and he wasn't sure why. Anxiety enveloped him. He felt terrible emotionally. However, Vic's wife was not only a mature woman. Her character was made of steel. She was a strong person who could handle even the toughest problems. This quality he had always deeply admired.

Instead of keeping his confusion to himself, Vic felt very safe in sharing his feelings with his woman. And he did. One evening, he opened up to his woman. And he did. One evening, he opened up to his woman. As he had expected, she was calm and reassuring. Her easy manner steadied him. She showed him deep understanding and lots of affection. It wasn't very long before Vic was feeling better and smiling again.

*****

When a man believes that his wife or beloved is capable of handling "bad news" and problems, he is more disposed to sharing his problem with her. If he believes she will not over-react to what he has to say to her, chances are that he will risk being open with her. If, on the other hand, he thinks that discussing unpleasant matters with her will only cause her to add to his problems, then he would have to be crazy to share.

Sharing, deep sharing, is the ideal in marriage and in friendship. However, reality is clearly not the ideal. The truth of the matter is that many spouses cannot deal with unpleasant news very well. They tend to panic. They seem to lose their objectivity and to exaggerate. They may worry more than their spouse. In the end, the man is faced with his *and* her worries. Confronted with his option, he would rather suffer less and withhold natters from his wife.

If a woman wants her man to be open with her, she must be sure to make the environment favorable for him to do so. Exerting a greater effort to stay calm; "acting as if" she were steady; showing him understanding while *effectively* pretending not to be bothered; all these postures help make a man feel at ease and more prone to be frank about his feelings.

THE TRAUMA OF SEPARATION

IT ALL HAPPENED so fast. They had been married 16 years. The three children were growing up and doing well in school. She had never doubted her love for him. And she felt that he loved her dearly. That was until, one day, she learned that he was having an affair with a much younger woman. She decided not to surrender her husband without a fight. She did everything in her power to hold on to him. However, it was all to no avail. He had fallen head over heels for the woman, and it was impossible to reason with him.

Finally, the day came when he broke the news to her. He was leaving her and the kids to set up house with his lover. He hoped she would understand. Of course, she didn't. But what could she do? There was bitterness, anger and resentment even as she bravely accepted the inevitable. The day he waved goodbye was, for her, like saying hello to a completely new lifestyle.

Now she was on her own. Although he helped out at first, it was never enough. After a while, his financial contributions to her and the children became erratic. She knew that sooner or later they would end. So she determined that she would have to support herself and work for the first time in her life.

It was scary in the beginning but, after a while her little buy and sell business prospered and she gained a whole lot of self-confidence. Earning enough was not a great problem. Handling the emotional void, the pain, the frustrations that accompanied the breakup was what drained her. And since it was necessary to put up a front for kids, the energy needed for this was tremendous. Pretending was not one of her strong points. However, she had little choice but to play along, for their sakes.

Getting into another relationship was surely out of the question. Even if there were a number of men, decent ones, who indicated an interest in knowing her better, she brushed them off without a second thought. She had been too hurt, too disappointed to consider another commitment so soon. With time, she might want to love and be loved again, but now it was her period of mourning and the time to give more attention to her children. Despite her aloneness, she succeeded quite well.

The trauma of a separation is difficult to deal with. Some spouses are shattered and take a very long time to recover. Others are quicker to react positively. There is something in them, in their character, which allows them to respond in a constructive manner,

However, whether or not one adapts well and quickly, the suffering is nevertheless there. And there is a need for healing. And healing takes time. If you have a friend who finds herself in that situation, you can help her by encouraging her to stand on her own and go on living. It won't be easy, but if you are persistent, you will experience great joy as she slowly picks herself up, shakes off the pain, and continues to make her way through life.

WHEN A WIFE IS A TREAT TO HER HUSBAND

SHE WAS A BEAUTIFUL woman. Tall and with a well-proportioned body, she was a striking person who turned the heads of men and women alike. Aside from her physical attributes, she was remarkably talented. She played the piano in an almost professional manner. She dabbled in art. She played a number of sports. And she was a career woman. She rose quickly in her company and now held a key position in a world of men. I guess you could describe her as quite a woman.

That was part of her problem. Although endowed with all these plusses, she was having difficulty findings and *keeping* the right man. Oh, getting dated was easy. There were more than enough offers for dinners, parties, etc. And men were always buzzing around her like flies pursuing sweets. There was, in spite of all of this, a deep frustration within her. Whenever a man would get to know her well, he would back away and leave her standing alone, wondering what had happened.

The truth is that some women are perceived by most men as highly threatening. Not physically, of course. When a man finds that his date is some kind of Wonder Woman, he naturally is at first taken aback. Then, after a while, he begins to compare himself to her. And, if he comes out a very distant second, that most often becomes cause for worry. No woman likes to feel inferior to a man. For a male to feel interior to a man. For a male to feel this way about a woman is even more terrible.

This is so because of social values which dictate that the man must be "macho" or at least the "strong one," the "protector" of his woman. When the roles are reversed, the situation becomes indeed very uncomfortable.

I remember a number of men who were married to women who "had all the money." These men could not help but feel bad about the fact that their wives were supporting them instead of the other way around. Our social values have been strongly ingrained in us. We cannot easily cast them aside.

Financial support is only one of many dimensions. The woman who is more mature, more intelligent, and more successful will pose a threat to her husband. This is one reason (never readily admitted to) why some men refuse to allow their wives to work or pursue activities that would cause them to develop more fully.

If a couple about to marry is caught up in this kind of situation, they have the perfect recipe for trouble. And the problem with this whole thing is that it becomes so hard for a man to acknowledge that truth that he feels threatened.

The bottom line in all is that not everyone can successfully handle a powerful personality. Not everyone can live comfortably with a woman who is a constant reminder of superior talent. Beauty, ability, intelligence and success often are the reasons for some men keeping their distance. Unless a man can feel inwardly comfortable with such a woman, he would do better to get a companion who is basically at his own level. He will be happier for it all.

ACCEPTING FACTS OF LIFE

SHE WAS A BEAUTIFUL woman in her mid-twenties. However, there was something sad about her bearing that made her seem less beautiful than she really was. Like a beautiful but drooping flower that makes you wonder what's wrong. You could sense that she had been to many battles and had come out of them alive, but not very well. She made you wonder what it was that had beaten her down so badly.

Pregnancy. She loved a man and had gone to bed with him. She was sure they would soon be married. He had promised her that match. When she told him she was with child, everything changed.

He gave her a hundred reasons he was unable to marry her now. It soon became clear to her that it would neither be now nor ever. There was a confrontation and although she expected him to say goodbye, she was deeply hurt when he walked away. It was as though he had stabbed her in the heart a thousand times.

There she was, cheated and alone. Well, not quite alone. There was life moving around in her belly. What to do about it was another question to be answered. At first, when she learned that she was pregnant, an immediate joy came over her because she felt that she would bear the fruit of their love. After he walked away, though, that joy turned into fear and a certain degree of despair. The child within her suddenly became very heavy indeed. She thought of destroying it, but she quickly fought off that kind of thinking. Was it her conscience, her instinct, her upbringing? I don't know, but she couldn't bring herself around to killing the life within her.

When the baby came, she was happy again, but her joy remained incomplete. After a while, bitterness began setting in and slowly poisoning her whole being. Whenever she met men, she saw in them the man who had betrayed her. Her response to them ranged from cold to indifference to irritation.

She kept her secret as well as she could, but the burden of it was so heavy that it exacted a heavy price. She lived in constant fear that new friends would learn about her child and then walk away from her. She felt deep shame about her past which caused her to hold back when she wasn't hiding.

After going through a lot of therapy, she began to accept the reality of her situation and live with it. She became convinced that keeping the child was an act of heroism in a society that is quick to condemn. There was newfound confidence as her self-image improved.

She began to smile and talked freely of her child to anyone who would listen. She was proud of the fact that she could speak so openly about something she feared terribly in the past. One day, she met a man who greatly admired her. When she told him about her child, he totally accepted her… child and all.

If you can accept yourself and be at peace with the realities of your life, you will soon learn that your self-acceptance makes it easy for others to accept you.

OLD FLAME

(This was my response to a letter written by a married woman still in love with her first love, who was also married and with children. Although they had not yet had sexual intercourse, they were seeing each other and were becoming intimate.)

YOU ARE ASKING ME if you should continue your affair with this man. I believe that is a question only you and should answer. After all, it's your life and not mine. It all depends on what it is you want, on what your convictions are, on whether or not you are willing to face the consequence of an affair.

Let's agree on one thing that is sure. There's no way you can go on with your affair indefinitely without people (and eventually your husband) learning about it. Please *don't* think you will be able to hide it forever. Someday, somehow, the truth will be known. And when that happens, all hell will break loose.

I know of many people who "enjoyed" their extramarital affairs as long as they remained secret. There was no hassle, no trouble. Only a lot of excitement, pleasure, and fantasy. However, when the affair became known by everyone, started talking about it, and the husband and the kids got angry and upset, the pressures and the strain became such that they found that the affairs was not worth the price tag attached to it.

So ask yourself the question: Is it really worth it? Are you so unhappy that you are willing to deal with the consequences of your affairs?

Some people are so desperate that they no longer care what happens. Others involved in affairs would quickly back away if they were sure to get caught. Having an affair is attractive to them, but only up to a point, only if they are not discovered.

If you really don't love your husband anymore, then you must be seriously thinking of leaving him. However, I don't see that in your letter. You really have few gripes against your man. I think you are, if anything, bored. And now that your old flame has popped into your life again, there is a newfound sense of excitement.

I must caution you about this affair, though. I believe there is a lot of fanciful fantasizing going on. You are imagining that had you married your old flame, things would have been very different. Maybe so. Perhaps you would be even more unhappy.

Right now, you are playing with fire. You are falling fast for this man. And unless you get out now, you will get in deeper. Unless you move away forcefully NOW, it is only a matter of time until you go to bed with him. When that happens, getting out will surely be many times more difficult.

Ultimately, the choice is yours to make. And, since you will have to face the consequences, it is only right that you be the one to decide.

I didn't mention the moral aspects of your affairs since you are a graduate of an exclusive school for girls. I don't wish to be repetitious and bore you with things you already know full well. God be with you in your decisions.

A MARRIAGE DOOMED TO FAIL

SHE WAS PRETTY, intelligent and desperate. She had been into a number of relationships before and none had worked out. Now she was beginning to think that she would never end up married. The thought of having to live alone frightened her terribly. And so, when he came buzzing around her, she grabbed him… and held on tightly.

It was a strange kind of courtship. People who knew them commented that she seemed particularly unenthusiastic about the whole thing. It was as if she were going through the motions without the usual feelings you would expect. As if she were saying: "Come on, let's get on quickly with the marriage."

Another thing. She had eyes for other men. In fact, to see her, one would not think that she was about to get married. Quite the contrary, it seemed that she was still looking back over her shoulders on her way to the altar. She surely did not give the impression that she was deeply committed to her fiancée. It was as if she was having second thoughts right up to the last.

Anyway, she got her wedding. And three children. Then came the breakup. Heavy conflict developed between them. She was always impatient with him. He irritated her. She felt he did not fulfill her needs. Then she no longer wanted to sleep with him. He tried to save the marriage. But nothing he did worked. And it did not work because there was little desire on her part to make it work. Finally, he gave up and started looking elsewhere. When he found another woman, she did not flare up. It was as if she felt a deep sense of relief. As if his affair officially put an end to their commitment to each other.

Now, she felt free to go her own way. And, before long, she too was caught up in her own affair. A while later, both agreed to say goodbye.

This was a marriage that should have never taken place. It was doomed to fail even before it got off the ground. It lacked commitment from the very beginning. Its level of maturity was too low to carry it through. The two were incompatible. And their love was too shallow to weather the inevitable storms that would surely arise. And, when the wind blew with gale force, and the waves rose, their ship broke up under the strain.

Marriage is easy to get into. Tough to get out, though, tough because the price in terms of pain, emotional hurt and frustrations is exceedingly high. Tough because you end up finding yourself back to square one. Even square minus one, they say that "love is better the second time around" Not always. However, if it does work out better the second time, there will be more complications, more problematic dimensions to deal with.

It will be a lot easier for all involved if things go right the first time. It is of prime importance that people be careful and think before making the fateful decisions to commit themselves to another for a lifetime. The consequence (medium and long term) of such a decision should be considered in detail. And, when in doubt, one should always postpone the wedding bells. Failure to do so could result in a decision that would be full of regrets down the road.

INCOMPATIBLE COUPLE

SHE WONDERED WHY her friends were so strongly opposed to her impending wedding. They seemed unanimously against it. Frankly, she could not understand why.

Of course he was jealous. But were not all men jealous? And was not jealousy a sure sign of a deep love?

She did not agree with her friends when they told her they thought that her fiancée was carrying his jealousy too far. In her mind, his possessiveness was due solely to the fact that he loved her with all his heart and simply did not wish to lose her. Besides, it felt good to be pursued with such passion and aggressiveness.

Her friends were also warning her about the imbalance that they perceived in their careers. She enjoyed mixing with all kinds of people. And she was good at it. The life of the party, she was a popular woman whose name could be found on everybody's invitation list. As a result of her preference for people, her job took her into the very midst of human beings where she proved to be very effective at interacting with them.

The man she loved and had every intention of marrying was very much her opposite. A technical man, he preferred solitude to the crowd. He did not aspire to achieve great things. He readily admitted that all he wanted was a quiet home life surrounded by kids and a faithful and loving wife.

Problem was that she was not the homebody type. She wanted very much to pursue her career. She remained very aware of the undeveloped potentials that remained locked within her. Consequently, she longed to actualize the potentials. Her career was important to her.

She was also a very independent type who resented her in-laws-to-be whenever they tried to interfere in her life and tell her what to do. However, she believed that sooner or later their love would overcome in-law problems and all the other would-be barriers about which everyone was warning her. Since her mind was already set, she really did not listen very much when her friends presented their views. They were well-meaning enough; however, the decision was hers to make, and she had decided to go ahead no matter what.

She married. Within a year, heavy conflict broke out between her and her husband. The issues were not at all new. She got tired of his excessive jealousy and possessiveness. She felt stifled as a person. She could not move without him suspecting her of being up to something.

When she insisted on going back to work after giving birth, there was intense conflict. She felt that his reasons for wanting to keep her at home were more than he was saying. She was convinced that he used the "take-care-of-the-child" issue as a smoke screen for his feeling of jealousy and his desire to keep her "out of circulation." She wanted to be among her friends. He thought she went out too much already.

The in-laws got involved. They argued about money. Tension and stress became constant companions. She felt she was going crazy. She wished she could turn back the hands of time, but she could not.

LOSING HER MAN

How does a dedicated and loving woman feel when she sees her husband slowly stepping out of her warm embrace and begin to move away?

I suppose I could only give you a very vague answer to the above question because it is too difficult to adequately describe feelings of pain on paper.

The wife who suddenly realizes that her man is no longer exclusively hers is besieged with many varied emotions. For many years, she had led a sheltered life in the confines of her home. She did not have to worry so much about tomorrow's breakfast because her husband saw to it that the family was amply provided for.

Now all that seems to have changed. Oh yes, the man still brings the bacon home, but the woman is no longer sure when he will walk out on her and the kids and leave them standing in the cold without the necessary means of support.

The woman who knows she is losing her grip on her man also worries about what people will say about her situation. Her pride is deeply wounded. She is losing ground to another female and that hurts beyond belief.

It's such a tremendous blow to her ego that we men find it practically impossible to understand. Women are not good losers. In fact, sportsmanship is not one of their strong points.

Loneliness is another characteristic of the woman who watches her man slowly drift out of her reach. Though her husband continues to come home (many times late in the evening) she feels alone. Though he sleeps by her side every night, she has a heavy losing ground to her competitor. And when her husband makes love to her, it is difficult to convince her that he is not thinking of the other woman.

She also feels cheated. After spending the best years of her life with him and bearing his children; after countless sacrifices (joy too!) and giving so much, she suddenly finds herself without any tangible return on her great emotional investment. She feels empty and bitter. It's a sad situation, but it's real. And it happens to countless people every day.

THE SAME BROKEN PROMISES

SHE KNEW BEFORE she married him that he was abusing drugs. She did not like it at all and told him so. He said that he loved her so much that he would give up his habit. He was so convincing that she believed him. That was her first and perhaps most fatal mistake.

She loved him so much that she wanted to believe that his love for her would be enough to make him stop. She went ahead and married him. That was the beginning of a seemingly endless chain of events that caused their relationship to sour. It soon became apparent that his words were empty. He went right on taking drugs. In fact, things got much worse. In time, he lost his job because of tardiness and absenteeism. Jobless, he lost heart. Instead of doing something of himself, he fell into deep depression and accelerated his drug usage.

By this time, the situation was swiftly deteriorating. His wife and child seemed to mean nothing to him. Even if they were completely neglected by him, he showed no guilt, no remorse. When, after a while, his wife urged him to do something about his condition or she would leave him, he panicked and promised to stop. But he insisted that he could do it all by himself. He did not need help from anyone. She believed him again. Another mistake.

After a couple of weeks, he was again back to his old ways. She was now desperate. A number of years had passed and it was as if their lives were centered around drugs and their dire consequences. Drugs! Drugs! Always the same story. Promises! Promises! Always the same broken promises. Beginning! Beginning! Always beginning and never being able to come to any conclusions. Always seeming to run around in circles. There was no progress. None whatsoever. If at all, they seemed to be going backwards. And she was tired, so tired. Her strength was being sapped by this never-ending problem. Her love for him had long ago eroded considerably. She wondered how long she could go on. In fact, she wasn't sure if she even *wanted* to go on. Finally, after six years of the same nightmare, she threw in the towel and gave up. When she left him, she could not shed a single tear. If anything, she felt a deep sense of relief, a kind of liberation.

When a woman gets stuck with a drug dependent, the chances of things working out are slim indeed. Not that there is no hope. There is. However, unless the man wants to help himself; unless he seeks help from those who can and are willing to come to his aid; unless his family strongly motivates him to change his ways; unless he gets into some kind of program that can focus on his weakness; unless all these ingredients are present, he will fail. So will his marriage. And this should come as no surprise to anyone.

TRAGEDY OF FORCED MARRIAGES

THEY WERE YOUNG, immature, and irresponsible. And they were courting. It was a fast kind of relationship, one that progresses quickly but without much depth. Before long, they went to bed. Shortly after, she became pregnant.

That was when everything exploded. Her family became very upset, angry, and anxious. He got scared. He liked her but did not love her. Surely not enough to marry her. He told her that. However, she felt very differently about the whole matter. She said she loved him. She wanted him badly. That is perhaps why she did not seem unduly concerned about her pregnancy. Almost as though she had secretly hoped it would happen.

Now she was pressing him to marry her. And her family joined in applying pressure. They talked to his parents in a not too gentle manner and reminded them of their son's obligations and responsibilities. Finally, things got rough. When he still refused to marry her, the girl's family threatened him. Afraid of physical harm, the young man finally conceded. He married her. Then, after a few weeks, he promptly left her.

One of the most tragic happenings is the forced marriage. When two young people (and the not-so-young) have sexual intercourse, things have gotten serious. When they are faced with an unwanted pregnancy, then matters have gone from serious to grave.

Not thinking of the consequences of their actions, they are now faced with an accomplished fact (pregnancy) that precipitates matters very swiftly and forces people to make lifetime decisions quickly and under tremendous pressures.

Under the most normal circumstances, marriage is a momentous decision. It calls for serious thinking and calm reflection. Because the consequences are so far-reaching, the decision to marry calls for deep thinking and careful analysis.

All this is forfeited when suddenly the woman is found to be with child. Because of the time element involved in the pregnancy, everyone is under pressure to decide what to do. Panic sets in. family members feel the stress that the impending shame will bring. People do NOT think long term. Instead, everyone is looking for short-term answers. And convenient answers. This is when marriage seems like the quickest and most acceptable solution.

By forcing a marriage to take place, the families are almost surely ensuring that there will be tremendous tension in that relationship right from the beginning. And instead of an initial period of peace, the first day of the honeymoon is marked by devastating tension, rising anger and bitter disappointment on the part of the one compelled to marry. The chances of this kind of marriage succeeding are extremely slim. It will take some kind of miracle to make it work.

A marriage that takes place under the best of circumstances has no built-in guarantee of success. There are too many hidden obstacles and traps. But the forced marriage is almost sure to fail. There are simply too many things going against it for it to succeed. In applying short-term answers to a long-term problem, parents are dooming the unfortunate couple to all kinds of trouble and pain in the future.

By the way, if it can be proven in a Church court that a marriage was forced, that is sufficient ground for an annulment.

IN A DIFFICULT SITUATION

AFTER FOUR YEARS of marriage, he was not happy. He felt as if the walls were closing in on him. His feelings had nothing to do with his career because he was rapidly advancing up the corporate ladder. Financially, he had more than enough.

What bothered him so much was his relationship with his wife. She was basically a good woman. If he had not seen the fine qualities in her, he would have never married her. She was a concerned mother and took good care of his children.

What was pushing him to the edge was her extreme possessiveness. And her jealousy. Both went hand-in-hand. It was as if she watched him day and night. She suspected him of cheating on her. He wasn't. No amount of reassurance on his part seemed to satisfy her. And the truth of the matter was that he had remained loyal to her since their wedding day. In fact, opportunities to play around had come his way. Every time, he had said no to his urges.

Yet, she had her way of hinting to him that perhaps he had not been faithful. Maybe he was thinking of having an affair. How come he enjoyed talking to that beautiful woman so very much? Did he think she was more attractive? Or more intelligent?

If he befriended someone, even a male, she felt threatened. Perhaps he would spend more time with his new friend and neglect her. Maybe he would care for him more than her.

On and on it went. Day after day, for months. And he was getting tired of it all. The stress was getting to him. He found it difficult to relax even at home. He became irritable with his children. He snapped at them for no reason at all.

Of course they fought. What else would you expect? And the more they argued, the more he moved away from her. And the more she sensed him slipping away from her, the more suspicious, the more jealous and the more possessive she became. And the more he reacted negatively.

Thus, they were caught up in a vicious cycle. Their frustrations grew as they seemed to be caught in an impasse. It looked like there was no way out. The seeming hopelessness of it all was getting to him.

He felt trapped. Like a tiger in a cage. And as the days passed, the pressure mounted. He felt he needed to break out, go crashing through the window if need be. But he had to get out. He felt he had no one to talk to. There were, of course, a number of people he could have approached, but somehow, he didn't. He kept it all in and, after a while, thought he would go crazy.

When a man (or a woman) finds himself in that situation, he is indeed in a difficult situation. And unless he gets some help from a competent counsellor, he may end up doing something drastic. Men caught up in such situations often beat their wives. They use their fists because they feel that nothing else will work. A little like the woman who, in frustration, throws things.

If the two of them are going to make it, they will need a lot of therapy. She to understand why she is as unreasonable as she is. He to understand her and learn to exercise more patience as she slowly makes some changes.

AFFAIRS ARE COMPLICATED

HE WAS A MARRIED man who had grown weary of his marriage. A kind of dullness and boredom had crept into his relationship with his wife. They hardly ever fought. But they did not love passionately either. It was as if they were just there in the house. Nothing exciting. Everything routine. Even their love life was no longer fun or pleasurable.

It was then that he met her. She was working in a bar. He frequented the place because he was looking for some kind of action.

She gave it to him. Before long, he had her set up in an apartment and was spending more time with her than at home. His wife did not want to rock the boat. She pretended she did not notice his long absences. She was afraid to lose him, although she had in effect already lost him.

He carried on with his affair for a long time. Finally, his wife could no longer bear it. She exploded. A terrible fight broke out. He left the house and moved into the apartment of the mistress. A year or so later, the wife died. No doubt, her broken heart had lessened her will to live.

His only son, barely twelve, moved in with his father. It was not long before conflict broke out between the boy and his father's woman. He talked back and showed a total disrespect of her. This, of course, irritated her to no end. After a while, she fought back.

One day, during one of those increasingly bitter verbal battles, he called her a whore. Enraged, she slapped him. When his father heard about the incident, he grew angry; he insisted that she apologize. She refused. More conflict.

She left the house. She was sure he would fetch her and bring her back. He didn't. When finally she returned to the house, he no longer wanted her. To this day, she blames the child for their separation.

No doubt, the boy blames her for the death of his mother. And chances are that the husband is keeping a lot of guilt feelings inside. There is unhappiness all around.

Affairs are complicated. Rarely are they simple and smooth. Usually, they are full of tension. The need for secrecy keeps up an endless amount of pressure on those who are trying to hide. Some of the most ordinary things become major projects. Going out to the movies is risky. Driving together is too. The couple into an affair is always looking back over the shoulder, worried about who is watching.

It is as though real relaxation is difficult to attain. This kind of existence puts a lot of heavy pressure on the couple. They have the usual problems that every couple has to contend with. Aside from these, there is that often unbearable pressure to contend with.

The complications that affairs give birth to are often beyond solution. It is as though there is no way out.

Before going beyond the point of no return, a man/woman needs to think about the costs of an affair. Unless one is willing to pay dearly, one had better think of other options.

BULLY IN MARRIAGE

THERE ARE TIMES in a marriage when one partner forgets that the contract he signed on his/her wedding day was one between equals. Not long ago, a young lady in her mid-twenties wrote to me about this particular problem. It seems that her husband has forgotten how to negotiate things and is resorting to outright dictatorship in the family. She says that she feels "suffocated" because of the way he handles her "in the sense that I'm always forced to obey him, though I believe things ought to be done the other way around."

What is tragic is that they had been married only a year or so and have a child. It looks like the trouble that has surfaced is not easily dealt with since it concerns an attitude. And attitudes are not quickly modified, much less changed.

As the man continues throwing his weight around, the bitterness and resentment build up in the wife's heart. It will continue to do so until the woman reaches her breaking point. Then we are going to be seeing a lot of fireworks.

The man who continuously pushes his wife around (women do it too) without getting a strong response from her may think he is married to a weakling. He may believe that no matter what happens, she will hang in there and bear with his bullying forever. He might be right. There are countless women who are martyred in this way every day of their lives. They suffer terribly but have the willingness and the emotional ability to handle the psychological beatings they regularly get from their spouses.

However, there are those who are not made of the same kind of fiber. These women are much more sensitive and delicate. They cannot take much manhandling without reacting to it. These are the ones who run home to their parents or who walk out and separate permanently. I guess, unless the man changes; the woman will be reduced to choosing to either hang in there or leave.

The man who thinks he has a martyr when his wife is really the other kind is going to get a terrible surprise when all hell breaks loose and she walks out on him.

I remember such a situation. The man had always given the orders in their marriage. When I warned him and told him that his wife was not the martyr type and was capable of saying goodbye, he merely laughed and said, with a tinge of arrogance: "she wouldn't dare." Well, she did dare. And when she walked away from him, he was totally shattered.

What is dangerous in this kind of situation is miscalculation on the part of the bully. Like the big guy on the block who picks on the little kid only to find too late that the small guy holds a black belt in karate. In the same way, the bully in marriage who has been used to getting his own way all these years rarely had the ability to handle, much less contain, the fury of the suddenly rebellious wife who has had enough. The consequence is usually a separation that remains permanent.

SUCCESS AND THE MARRIED WOMAN

SHE HAD BEEN WARNED by friends before the wedding. It seems so clear to them that somehow their marriage would not work out. Yet, she was sure that it would. How could it fail? They loved each other so very much... more than anyone could ever know. He was such an understanding man.

In fact, he had encouraged her in her professional career. Her friends had told her that her job would eventually become a problem for him. She was more talented, had greater potential, and had a much brighter tomorrow. That worried her friends. They did not think that he could handle her future success. They believed that it would somehow get to him. He would react and conflict would break out.

They were correct. The first years of marriage were beautiful and relatively conflict-free. They were at about the same point as far as their careers were concerned. Then she began to pull ahead. One promotion. Then another. She was leaving him behind in prestige and in earning power. He began to resent her success in a very subtle manner. He never told her directly. However, he was now urging her to quit her job and stay home and be a simple housewife. He had felt this way before. Even if they would take a substantial loss in earnings, he was ready to accept it. What mattered was that she quit her job.

What he refused to accept was the possibility that he was feeling threatened by her success. There was no way that he was ready to admit to that. In reality, he could not bear watching her streak ahead of him professionally. She made him look so small, so inferior. Her salary was three times his. She was acknowledged as a leader in her field while he was bringing up the rear. His resentment slowly and silently grew in intensity until one day there was an explosion. The question of whether or not she should quit became a burning issue between them.

Finally, she learned that he was having an affair with another woman who happened to be his subordinate. If one were to compare his wife and his mistress, there was nothing to really compare. His wife stood head and shoulders above his lover. And perhaps that is the way he wanted it. He has in effect totally reduced the competition. With his wife out of the picture (he separated from her) he became the dominant figure in his new relationship. There was no way his new woman could outshine him. He felt a whole lot more secure. And he liked the feeling.

His wife finally accepted the fact that she would never be free to grow as long as she gave in to him. She needed a more successful man who would not react negatively to her success because he had more than enough of his own to satisfy him. It took a while for her to get over the trauma of separation. However, after the wounds had healed, she realized that it was better this way. She would make her own way through life. She would walk a new road. It scared her in a way, but she believed enough in herself and in His loving kindness to face the future with a smile.

THE COUPLE WHO COULDN'T SEEM TO COME TO TERMS

THEY HAD BEEN COURTING for more than four years. A young, attractive couple, they had told their friends and family that they planned to marry soon. However, he was beginning to have a number of doubts about the whole relationship. The thoughts of an impending marriage became less and less appealing and more and more scary. He felt as though he was being pushed into a corner and he did not like it.

She was the strong, aggressive type of woman. At a very early age, she had tasted success. Rising from the ranks, she became a vice-president before her 25th birthday. She had earned the reputation for getting things done quickly and efficiently. She knew she could accomplish a lot more in business and loved her work. She had a way of translating her unusual drive in business into her relationship. She loved with a fury. In fact, her kind of loving would overwhelm most men. There was an intensity, a quality about it that made it difficult for a man to respond in a like manner. Her loving was all-consuming and left little room for compromise and flexibility. She expected her man to love her the way she loved him.

It was her expectations of him that put enormous pressure on him. He just could not seem to handle it. Shae came across to him as pushy. And perhaps she was. She wanted the date for the wedding to be announced. She was working to have them buy a house and lot. He was dealing with a powerful woman and he knew it. And it bothered him.

He was a different kind of man. He did not aspire after great success. Only enough to satisfy his needs. He longed for a quiet family life, a wife who would stay at home and take care of her husband and children. He wanted peace, serenity and predictability. He was beginning to doubt that she could and would give it to him.

His doubts arose from what he saw was happening to them. They were constantly getting into arguments over some basic values and convictions. It was as if they were pulling in opposite directions because of differing needs. They could not seem to come to terms. She wanted to pursue her career. He wanted her to be a family woman. She longed to explore new and exciting challenges. He preferred a more quiet, sedate kind of living. Her love was all-encompassing, all-enveloping. He felt overwhelmed and wanted space to move around in. She was dedicated and loyal, but possessive. He needed to feel a greater sense of freedom.

As the pressures and tensions from argumentation and conflict grew, he decided to seek counsel. After a long session that was amazingly quiet and sensible, the two of them decided to separate. They still loved each other, but their minds told them that continued conflict would, in time, erode the love they now felt for each other. So, they decided to part ways as friends. They hugged and kissed each other and embraced me before leaving my home.

As they walked away into the dark night, I marveled at their maturity and balance. Did they do the right thing? I believe so. Will they have regrets? I doubt it. Will they be better prepared for their next love? Definitely!

HARD REALITIES

THE FOLLOWING IS basically a true story. Some of the circumstances have been changed in order to protect those involved. However, it is a story that bears telling because it is not uncommon. And perhaps a number of my readers will identify with it and be helped.

She is young (in her thirties), married with children. In the beginning of her marriage, she was ecstatically happy with her husband. However, the pursuit of their careers forced them to spend lots of time away from each other. That was not a problem for her. It was for him, though. Eventually, he got involved with another woman.

At first, she knew nothing about it. Later on, a friend told her. She was shattered. She decided to fight for her husband and did everything to get him back. He never really admitted to having an affair, but she knew the truth. He was discreet and careful but still she was able to catch him every once-in-a-while.

For a long time, they played their cat-and-mouse game. Of course, she was deeply hurt and felt rejected. And the stress and tension in her life were tremendous.

After some time, she ran into a man who told her he loved her. At first, she did not respond. Then, after a while, she "felt compelled" to respond to him. It was as if her feelings were so strong that she could no longer control herself. He was also married and before she knew it, they were having a full-blown affair.

Her conscience and her moral values told her what was happening was wrong. She wanted to pray to God for help, but she was afraid to do so. He might answer her prayer and she would lose her lover. And she did not want that to happen. Not at all.

The more she fell in love with her lover, the more she had to face the truth about her relationship with her husband. She had to admit to herself that she really no longer loved him the way she used to. She also believed that his love for her had fallen to an all-time-low.

Now she was faced with a very complicated situation. Her marriage, her children, her lover, his family, etc. That was when I knew her. What I told her was simple. She would have to come to grips with reality. Otherwise, things would spin out of control and get awfully messy. She would have to face the truth about her marriage. She would have to decide whether or not she wanted to try to save her marriage. And if she did decide to try to save it, would her husband feel the same way? Was there still enough love between them to make a go of it?

And if her marriage was finished, then she would need to turn her attention to her affair. Was there deep love between them? Or were they both simply needing each other? How would the future work out for them? What impact would their affair have on their respective families, their careers, and their standing in their community?

Lots of questions needing lots of answers. Lots of hard realities to face up to. And only she could initiate action. If she stood by and let things happen, the final outcome would be anybody's guess.

HUSBAND CAUGHT IN A TRAP

WHEN AN ANGRY letter writer commented on the slaying of the mistress of a man by his wife, she was full of feelings. "My sympathy," she wrote, "goes to the wife, not to the slain woman." Evidently, she believed that the dead mistress got what she deserved.

What is strange is that nothing is said about the husband who was fooling around. The blame is heaped upon the mistress and not the husband who is a lot older, should be a lot more mature and wiser, and should know better. It is assumed that the man is weaker and easily seduced by the mistress.

The truth of the matter is that men seduce women more often than women seduce men. What about prostitutes and hospitality girls that abound in the city? Well, these women have their haunts and hangouts. They do not have the run around looking for men to seduce. Men willingly go to them to be seduced. In this case, the men are the willing victims.

When a married man is attracted to a young lady, he is the one who usually makes the first move and not vice-versa. He is the one who makes the approaches and weaves his web around the girl. I am sorry, but I do not give these young ladies all that much credit for their seductive skills. I believe men (especially older men) are better at the art of seduction than women. The man who does not want to get caught will almost never get caught by a woman. Why? Because he will be careful not to expose himself in ways that will set himself up for an affair. He will avoid bar girls. If he senses that a young lady likes him, he will be careful not to allow himself to stray into an environment that is conducive to the birth of an affair. In other words, he will show great agility in sidestepping traps that could set him up for an affair.

The problem. Though. is that almost all men who get into affairs are not trying hard enough to avoid them. And, a great majority of them are actually ready and waiting and willing to jump into one the moment the scenario for an affair begins to unfold. Because they are no longer happy in their marriages, they have one eye cast across the fence looking for greener pastures. Or maybe their relationship with their spouses has become stale, unexciting and boring. Or, perhaps they are simply looking for something to get into because they sense that their marriage is not enough to satisfy their needs.

Whatever the case may be, I am of the strong conviction that the man is just as much to blame as the woman he was an affair with. And perhaps more so. To wish evil and misfortune on the mistress and exonerate the man or limit his liability in the matter is unfair.

IF THERE'S LOVE, THERE'S TRUST

The other day, a couple consulted me about a problem. Actually, it wasn't really a problem at all; it was a problem they created.

It seems that the guy visited his girlfriend in her house. He got hurt very badly when she didn't even come down and he had to be entertained by her mother and sister. He felt that she deliberately snubbed him. The truth of the matter was that the young lady lay exhausted and asleep the whole time and wasn't even aware of his presence in the house.

The man, however, would not accept her explanation and thus the problem. It all came down to whether or not he believed her story. In the end, all went well, and they walked away arm in arm because they were able to iron out their differences.

The point I would like to make in this column is that the overwhelming majority of the arguments and hurt feelings in love and marriage could be avoided if only people would not be so quick on the trigger. It is a rule of the woods that while hunting a man should be sure that his target is an animal and not a human being. Hundreds of hunters are killed every year because some trigger-happy, nervous individual fired pointblank into a clump of moving bushes.

Likewise, untold damage is done to lovers and spouses everywhere by thoughtless people who fire off all kinds of irresponsible statements before knowing the facts. Have you noticed how two people arguing over something really and truly agree in substance more often than not? The truth is that they differ mostly in the way they express the same thought.

People who don't like to listen to all the facts are more likely than anyone to get into all kinds of trouble. Not because they are lacking in sincerity or goodwill. It's just that they don't know the whole story and are likely to misunderstand.

Finally, if a man doesn't really love a woman (or his friend), he will most likely not want to believe her anyway. If there is deep love, there is deep trust — a lot fewer chances of misunderstanding each other.

"LOVE TRIANGLE"

A WOMAN WROTE to me and asked me to write "about what a drifting-away husband feels when found out by the dedicated and loving" wife of his affair with "another woman." There is usually a heavy conflict that breaks out when the whole thing comes to light. All hell breaks loose as the pain and sufferings of the woman rise to the surface.

"How," she wrote, "does he stand on the other side? Can he readily give up his new love? Can he keep his promise to his wife that the affair is all over? Women in this situation cannot accept another lie. They are most cautious and protective of their wounded and pained feelings. Though they may forgive, they cannot easily forget."

Good questions and insightful observations too. Of course, there are no easy answer because I am not familiar with the details of this case. Can he readily give up his new love? That depends on a number of factors. The intensity of his love for his mistress. The level of his love for his wife. If he no longer loves his wife but has deep feelings for his mistress, I would bet that his promises of giving her up are empty words.

Another factor will be the responses of both the wife and the mistress. Does the wife nag? Does she threaten to leave him? And, if she does, are hers empty threats? Does she create nasty scenes? Or does she give him the impression that no matter how often he is unfaithful, she will stand by him?

Is the mistress one of those women who threaten to make it difficult if he leaves her? Is she the "clinging" type who will cry and moan and attempt to make him feel "guilty," or is she the kind of woman who will give him up without a fight?

All these are just a few of the possible factors that might have an influence on the man's ability or willingness to walk away from his mistress. And the kind of person he is also important. How he reacts to situations is of vital importance in determining his final response.

What is important to remember though is that if the husband has developed a deep emotional as well as sexual involvement with his mistress, you can be sure that giving her up will not be easy. Remember that he carried on the affair in the first place because he liked it and found it to be beneficial to him. Men are not forced into affairs. They have them because they are convinced that there is something in it for them. Especially if they are worried and have children, a career, and a name to protect. To risk losing all this for an affair, a man *has* to know there is something in it for himself. Otherwise, he would not see the logic of getting involved in the first place.

If he loves his mistress deeply, it will be just as difficult for him to forget her as it would for you or me to wipe out the memory of a beloved. If she (the mistress) loves him just as deeply, then you can perhaps imagine how much harder it will be for him to break away permanently.

Besides, do you believe the man would have broken up the affair he had not gotten caught? I doubt it. And, if he was perfectly willing to go on indefinitely before being discovered, I would have to doubt his willingness to give up the mistress even after the affair comes to light.

A MISMATCHED MARRIAGE

SHE WAS A BEAUTIFUL woman. Beautiful in every way: physically, intellectually and emotionally. She possessed an unusually attractive and pleasant personality. Warm and affectionate, she was capable of loving intensely and completely. Intellectually stimulating and psychologically mature, she was any man's dream woman.

One man was lucky enough to win her heart. They were married. However, soon after the honeymoon, the trouble began to set in. he was no match for her. Beset with a number of emotional hang-ups and insecure in many ways, her man soon became difficult to live with. Highly immature, he had difficulty agreeing with the more responsible behavior of his wife. It was not very long before their lives settles into a pattern of routine and repeated conflicts that would somehow never seem to get resolved. But she was a strong woman with a high stress level. She tolerated his childish behavior for years. Children were born and grew up.

However, as time passed and her frustrations grew in number and intensity, her respect for him began to disappear. And when the level of respect falls, the level of love drops in direct proportion. By the time she got to me, her mind was just about made up. She had decided to say goodbye. And she did.

The question that kept running around in my mind was this: how did such an emotionally healthy woman end up living with such an emotionally unhealthy man? Why did such a mismatch occur?

I suppose the answer is multi-dimensional and there is no one factor that could adequately describe what happened. Surely, the intensity of their young love had something to do with blinding her to some hard realities about her man. Even the immature and the irresponsible can be lovable in some ways. Her own lack of deep awareness factor. In the beginning, she failed to understand the grave consequences of his behavior.

Then there was her optimism. She was so sure that everything could be worked out somehow. She did not believe that some situations in marriage cannot be resolved and that the only answer lies in a choice between martyrdom and separation.

Her kindness was another factor. She possessed so much goddess that she could not turn her back and walk away while they were still courting. She pitied him and she failed to realize that pity is a treacherous foundation for marriage. It almost always is a destructive element in any love situation.

Although she showed great strength throughout the many years of her marriage, there *was* a limit to what she could and would endure. Even strong women have a breaking point. Even they reach a point where they feel that walking away from it all is the only rational thing to do.

TIRED OF GIVING AND TAKING?

EVER SINCE I WAS a boy, I have heard countless people say: "Love (or marriage) is give and take."

That expression has always made me feel uncomfortable. There is something about the word "take" that I have never liked because it implies violence. We say things like: "Next time, ask—don't just take without permission… the hijackers took over the airplane and occupied it for two hours…."

When you use the word take, there is that element of force in it that is quite clearly understood. I could never see where that word could fit into the picture with love. It always seemed so contradictory to me.

Oh, I understand what people mean. What they are trying to say is that in every love relationship, there must necessarily be some concessions on both sides. In short, when you're in love, you can't always have your own way. That may be so. However, I see this way of expressing it as negative thinking.

I look at love as a great contest between two people to see who gives more. If you and I are truly in love, I will do my best to out-give you. I will not count the gifts I have received from you as much as I will go out of my way to give you all that I have to give. You won't have to come forward and take anything because I will go to you and give you everything. In this way you are not taking, you're receiving. And as you very well know, there is a great difference.

And when you receive so much from me, your feelings are deeply touched and your heart is stirred to life and you feel like giving in return. This you do with lots of enthusiasm. Now I'm on the receiving end. I am so happy and impressed with your giving that my heart is stimulated to give more in return. And so it goes on and in an ever-widening circle and at an ever growing intensity.

Meanwhile, my head tells me that this relationship is good for me and very worthwhile continuing. And so my mind searches for ways and means to deepen the whole affair.

However, the moment one of us stops giving, then we're in trouble. Because I'm not receiving anything from you, my head tells me that my own emotional investment is no longer worthwhile. Consequently, I admit to the family of the whole thing and take my emotional investments elsewhere.

We all get tired of "giving and taking." But we never get fed up with giving and receiving.

WHEN INFIDELITY BECOMES ATTRACTIVE

He was a loyal family man and a good husband. Faithful to his wife from time to time he married her, he upheld the highest standard of marital fidelity. She was as loyal and as faithful as he, and as loving. They got along well. Doing many things together, thinking alike in numerous areas.

However, there were those moments when he looked past the beautiful relationship they enjoyed. There were times when his thoughts wandered off the well-worn path of fidelity. Although he was careful not to act on these thoughts and feelings, he was troubled because of them. And there was a measure of guilt present as he sometimes fantasized about other women.

These experiences happened especially during those times when for some reason or other, he was denied the satisfaction of his sexual needs. Either she was too tired or not in the mood. Or, perhaps, they had experienced some minor conflict. These were moments when he would find himself thinking of other women. No one special. Just women in general.

The above happens to countless people every day. Good individuals who are basically happy in their marriage. Men who do not want to have affairs because they love their wives and wish to maintain harmony in the family. Men who live by strict code of ethics.

Yet, needs are needs, whether they be emotional, psychological or sexual. The existence of these needs cannot be denied. Their satisfaction, though, is not always fulfilled. And when a need (any kind of need) remains unfulfilled or only partially satisfied, there will be consequences that will affect the well-being of a person.

In the case of the man (the woman too) whose sexual needs remain uncared-for, there will surely be some kind of longing, conscious or unconscious, that will cause tension and anxiety to surface. This is sometimes expressed in anger that comes out "sideways." The husband is irritable for no apparent reason. He is jumpy and quick to criticize people, things, and circumstances that never seemed to bother him before. Or he may rebel by "going out with the boys," or coming home late. All the better if his wife worries. That's what he wants. To get back at her somehow.

If the sexual needs of the husband go unfulfilled for an extended period of time, many things could happen. He might keep his tensions to himself and simply bear them, in which case bitterness is almost always a consequence. Or, he may do more than toy with the idea of having a "limited affair" in which he would not get emotionally involved. Because he is reaching his breaking point, fidelity is no longer as reasonable nor as attractive as it once was. He feels his way because his emotions enter the picture in a more intense fashion and block out some of the thinking process that allows for a more objective point of view.

The greatest danger of all is for him to become completely "turned off" by his wife's inability to fulfill his sexual needs. Because he believes that she never will, he is faced with the prospect of either remaining faithful and wanting sexually the rest of his life, or fooling around and achieving some degree of satisfaction. Under these circumstances, infidelity becomes much more attractive.

Please, let's not forget that everything I have said about the sexually unfulfilled man applies to the sexually needy wife, too.

DYING LOVE...

I MET A VERY miserable woman. She has been married to a man for years now. What is sad is that her love for him died a long time ago.

In spite of it all, she has continued to exist (I don't call it really living) with this man under the same roof because of social pressure (What will they say?), for the sake of her children "(I love my kids"), and because of fear and her feeling of insecurity ("How will I survive?")

I keep bumping into so many similar tragic situations. It seems that there are countless wives caught up in an unfortunate web of events that have caused them to live out their lives in unbelievable sorrow.

These women spend their time dreaming of ways to get out. But their dreams are never realized because it takes so much courage to come to a decision in these matters.

If the woman finally decides to stick it out with her husband through hell and high water, she is condemning herself to a life of misery characterized by a deep feeling of unfulfilled personal needs. It's like signing her own emotional death warrant. And even for "the sake of the children," this is no easy thing to do. It takes guts and strong, steady courage that must be translated into an everyday happening. All of us are brave sometimes. But not everybody can be brave all the time. It may be asking too much... more than some people can give.

If, on the other hand, the wife decides to leave her husband, she is faced with the same need for courage and determination. All these years she has been dependent on her husband for financial support (the emotional support has long been gone) and the prospect of going off on her own is indeed frightening.

The thought of what people might say is another very real factor difficult to face. People, taken as individuals, are nice. But as a whole society can be very nasty, cold, and heartless.

Then she must think of her kids. How will they react to her decision? Will they understand her or reject her?

Whatever such an unhappy wife decides, she is in for a lot of suffering. She has to get hurt. There is no possible way to avoid it. The most we people standing on the sidelines can do is give her active support in whatever decision she makes. The very least we can do is to stand by in polite silence, appreciate her difficult situation, and allow her the freedom from that destructive criticism that can strike paralyzing fear into the heart of the bravest of the brave.

BREAKING THE CYCLE OF SILENCE

THERE ARE TIMES in a marriage or a friendship when two people get into a series of misunderstandings that lead to conflict. Hard works are exchanged, hard feelings created. The level of anger and hostility mounts steadily. Both people begin to feel increasingly threatened by each other. Both feel a great deal of frustration at being unable to make themselves understood.

Finally, war is declared. A war of silence. One decides to stop talking, to give the silent treatment. The other is hurt and offended, and subsequently begins to play the same game.

Now, we have two adults indulging in child's play. Pride enters the picture and things become even more difficult. It is now a question of who will give in to whom. Life becomes unbearable in the house. He is angry and does not want to talk. She is also upset but would like to get a dialogue going because she realizes that this kind of behavior can badly damage their love. But, "she has her pride," so she also cooperates and plays the silent waiting game. The anger and the hostility continue to build up in an ever-increasing intensity. And since there is no attempt to diffuse it and to diminish it, it grows by geometric proportions until a real honest-to-goodness crisis is at hand.

The longer this kind of situation continues, the more difficult it is to undo it and to deal with it effectively. Both people feel that they have been pushed into a corner and have their backs against the wall. Neither one of them is very well disposed to receiving good feelings from the other. The sincerity and credibility levels at this time are exceedingly low, since this is not the kind of behavior that promotes sincere goodwill.

If there is to be any kind of reconciliation, someone has to break the brooding cycle of silence. Until and unless this is done, there is no way that things can possibly get better. On the contrary, there is a real danger that such circumstances could lead to at least a temporary separation.

Sometimes, a third party volunteers to come in and tries to re-establish lines of communication. If he enters the conflict uninvited, most likely he will fail and perhaps even aggravate the situation. If, however, both parties are willing to allow him to become a bridge between them, then the chances of success are greatly enhanced. Any couple that can settle on one and the same person to act as their bridge is fortunate.

If, however, there is no third party available or acceptable to both sides, one of the two is going to have to decide to make the first step. It will be an expensive one. The cost in terms of pride will be great. If, however, neither one is humble enough to make that first move, then, the cost in terms of love will be infinitely greater.

OPTIONS A BETRAYED WIFE MAY CONSIDER

WHEN A WIFE DISCOVERS that her man is having an affair with another woman, there are several options she can consider.

She can think of separation. This is, of course, a very drastic step. Many women give this option some serious thought. And why not? The aggrieved wife feels she has been betrayed, and she has. She has remained loyal to him for years; she has served him faithfully, she bore him children, and stood by him in times of crisis. And now, she feels the knife in her back. She has been cheated. Her pain is difficult to describe. The thought of leaving is easy for a man to understand if only he asks himself how he would feel if he learned that his wife was carrying on an affair with another man. Few men would not at least think of leaving.

However, the thought of leaving never crosses the mind of many women. Perhaps it is because, in spite of everything, these women have come to terms with an unpleasant situation and have made the decision to live with it all. The wife who suffers without *doing* anything is trying to avoid scandal. Or maybe she feels that rocking the boat will "affect the children." More often than not, she may be worrying about what will happen to her financially if ever there is a separation. If she has little or no means of supporting herself and her brood, it is scary for her to even think of leaving her husband.

What follows is a tragic scenario. The wife is miserable. If her husband continues his affair and she feels helpless to do anything about it, then she becomes angry and bitter in her own resigned way. Few women can handle such a situation by going on as if nothing happened. Not many can take it inwardly, although outwardly they maintain a calm and seemingly unbothered manner. But this is only an act. She knows it. Those who are aware of the true state of things know it too. She is not fooling anyone. Her marriage is in trouble and all the acting and pretending and looking the other way will do nothing to change this.

What can a woman do aside from leaving him or suffering hopelessly? She can get him into meaningful counselling. But what if he does not want to even think of going to a competent counsellor? The man in this kind of situation will, more often than not, avoid counselling like the plague. Perhaps it is because he is intelligent enough to know that counselling may force him to choose. And, right now, choosing is the farthest thing from his mind.

In this case, the woman should, in my opinion, begin to apply some pressure on him. She should let him know that he will have to pay dearly for his affair; that things will *not* be the same for him either; that she will not be alone in her suffering; that he also will have his share of unpleasantness. The man who is having an affair and who believes he can do so with impunity will only be encouraged to go on. If the price becomes increasingly difficult to bear, he might just review the value of his affair and come to the conclusion that it simply is not worthwhile.

The purpose of the pressure is to drive him into counselling, where some kind of progress might be made and where the stalemate might be broken. Unless some pressure is applied, the situation will result in a terrible dead end. What kind of pressure? I cannot say because I do not know the persons involved. It should not be given in anger and open hostility because that would only serve to make a reconciliation that much more difficult later. It should be applied gently but firmly in such a way that the husband will slowly but surely get the message that he cannot have his cake and eat it too.

SILENT TREATMENT

THIS IS GOING to be a very difficult topic because it is seldom discussed in newspapers and, in society, is only talked about in whispers and behind closed doors.

I know some people will be offended and will criticize me for daring to bring up the subject. However, I have met many married couples who have confided this problem to me. I feel there must be many out there I have not talked to who could be helped by what I have to say here. And what I have to say is meant primarily for you married women out there and those females among you who are contemplating to live with a man for the rest of your days.

When a man and a woman bind themselves together in marriage, they are doing just that—trying each other up for a lifetime. Hopefully, it will be a joyful, fulfilling captivity. However, there are times when the wedding bells end up sounding the death knell of what was once a beautiful love relationship.

When conflict in marriage begins to make itself felt, almost anything can happen. And when two people are angry at each other, there is no limit to the varied ways and means at hand with which to hurt. There is the "silent treatment." Then there is always the destructive word or phrase. Or one can always nag, or one can dig into the past and come up with an old skeleton, etc.

Another method, sometimes very effective, which wives often use to show their displeasure and/or to get even with the husband is the woman's refusal to have sexual intercourse with her spouse.

So many wives do not realize that sex means a great deal more to a man than it does to women. I also believe that a great number of wives know fully well how important sexual intercourse is to a man. And, because they know this, they withhold their sexual participation in order to gain the leverage they are looking for. Or perhaps to punish the husband for a real or fancied offense.

Many men have been rejected sexually by their wives after an argument. In a way, I feel sorry for the couple. Sexual intercourse is just about the most intimate and meaningful act two people can perform if there is a real meeting of hearts and minds.

Men very often try to make up for hurting their wives by making love to them. Some women very tragically repulse their husbands as though they had the plague. I call it a tragedy because most of the time, the woman really wants to put an end to the argument and misses an excellent opportunity to do so.

Perhaps it is because a wife who is hurt does not believe that her husband is really sincere but is just passionate and desires only to satisfy himself. This may or may not be true.

One thing, though, is certain. If a woman wants to really frustrate her husband, she can surely do so by refusing his advances. She can safely do this if the guy is highly principled. But if he isn't, then she can expect a few left turns on the road up ahead if she denies once too often. Remember, ladies, most men can have sexual relations with a woman and not love her one bit. You may not think of going to another man for sexual gratification if you cannot have it from your husband. Ordinarily, women are not prone to be intimate with men they do not love. Not so with men.

What I am trying to say is this: if a woman is looking for a chance to clear up a misunderstanding with her hubby, the time during the act of love is thought by many authorities to be the best. A man is more apt to listen and to be tender and receptive on this occasion. A woman who is well-meaning and concerned with solving her differences with her husband will be attentive to the most convenient conditions that will bring about a reconciliation. She will not let pass an excellent opportunity because of pride or revenge.

Some women throw the boomerang at their husbands, hoping to score a direct hit. What happens, more often than not, is that the boomerang comes right back and hits them squarely in the face.

THE HAUNTING PAST...

HE WAS A MAN who did not like to spend. He saved much of his income. He could have lived a luxurious life, but he did not. He preferred to put it away in case of a rainy day. When he thought about why it was like that with him, the poverty of his childhood came to mind. He never wanted to be poor again. He never again would go without. This concern was the prime motivating factor behind the ease with which he was able to save.

The pretty young wife had a problem with sex. Whenever her husband touched her and tried to make love to her, she became tense. And when they talked about it, she admitted that she did not like it. In fact, she secretly resented him and thought of him as a man with a dirty mind.

When she finally got help, it became clear to her why she felt this way. When she was a little girl, an uncle had put his hands on her. This incident traumatized her. Then, as an attractive teenager, she was the victim of an attempted rape.

She viewed men as always out to take her body. And when the man she loved became passionate and sexually aroused, she unconsciously saw in him her uncle and the man who almost raped her. It was tragic. What was supposed to be an act of love became something that alienated her from her man. The intimacy that was supposed to increase their love was taking it apart.

Just two examples of how the past is never truly forgotten. Nor is it insignificant. Whether we like it or not, whether we want it or not, whether it benefits us or not, the truth remains that our past *always* has an impact on the present.

In a friendship or a love relationship, it is absolutely essential that people understand some of the reasons for the behavior of a beloved. The wife who wants to spend more and cannot understand why her man has such an obsession with saving will be unhappy. And her relationship will be full of tension. If ever she comes to terms with her husband's hang-up, she will then be more at peace and this newfound understanding and acceptance will immediately be translated into her relationship. There will be more harmony

Similarly, the man who cannot understand why his wife is shying away from his sexual advances can become terribly hurt if he never understands why things are so. Unless he can piece together her past and make some sense out of it all, her behavior will remain a perplexing mystery to him. And the pain that her actions cause him will simply go on increasing and putting stress on their relationship until such time as the pressure gives rise to all kinds of conflicts that neither of them really wants.

Bob Garon

We are the sum total of our past. All of it. We are marked by events that may have faded from memory. We are greatly influenced by our actions and the actions of others in our past. To admit to this truth makes it easier for us to understand ourselves. To deny it is to turn a blind eye to reality.

THE DEVOTED WIFE

THEY HAD BEEN married for more than 20 years. She has always been a faithful and loving wife, a wonderful mother, and a very efficient homemaker. For long years, she has devoted herself completely to her husband, her family and her home. Countless times, she had sacrificed her own interest and pleasure because they conflicted with her priorities. It was difficult to find a more dedicated and unselfish woman.

He clearly did not deserve such a woman. Immature and irresponsible, he brought all kinds of suffering and pain upon his family. He drank too much, too regularly. He also gambled just as regularly. As if this wasn't enough, he also had an endless string of affairs with every conceivable kind of woman. He was insensitive to the hurt feelings (his vices were no secret) of his wife and children. All their pleas, cajoling, and appeals were like water running off a duck's back.

He was almost arrogant in the practice of his vices, and there was nothing anybody could do to reach him. His wife was a classic example of the martyr who bears it all, bleeds internally, and goes on "doing what's right."

He knew that she was such a highly principled woman, that she would never abandon ship (his ship) and, because he was well aware of this, he thoroughly abused her goodness, her kindness, and her principles.

This went on for many years until one day, when it all came to an end. It wasn't that he reformed or was converted but he acquired a serious kind of sickness. He became so sick that even if he wanted to continue, he couldn't. That was when things changed at home.

Now, our magnificent Casanova lost his desire for sex. Serious illness does something to the sexual urge. The doctor ordered him to stop drinking and he felt too sick to go out with his friends. His faithful wife turned all her attention on him. She took care of him as a mother tends to her sick child. It was as if he had never abused her. Slowly, almost grudgingly, he began to show her respect and affection but the sincerity of his attention was questioned by those who knew him. They felt that his sudden burst of love came about more because of his need for her than anything else. Deep in her heart, she somehow knew this to be true.

She went on caring for him, living him and attending to him, but it could have been a much more meaningful, a much more beautiful relationship, if only the painful past had not hurt so much. There was a kind of last minute sense of urgency that brought them together. Of course, he tried to make up. However, there was forced into this "newfound love," there was a ring of shallowness to it all. Somehow, it just did not seem true or right.

In a way, he was a lucky man. Fortunate that he had such a wonderful wife. Most women would have abandoned him long before. However, as always, "the chickens sooner or later will come home to roost." It is only a question of time before a man's past catches up with him.

GIVING WITHOUT HAVING

A BEAUTIFUL WOMAN is a pleasure to behold. A beautiful woman with the emotional reactions of a child is a pleasure to behold but difficult to live with.

When a woman discovers that her new husband, her handsome man, is childish in his ways, demanding and hardly ever aware of her feelings, then disillusionment sets in.

And if, God forbid, spouses are infantile in their reactions to marital differences, then their marriage is surely in trouble from the very start. When the wife is hurt and has a temper tantrum and goes off into a corner to pout; when she uses emotional blackmail by saying: "if you don't do this my way, then I know you don't love me"; when she refuses to engage in lovemaking with her husband because of her anger; when she goes into a deep silence and will not talk about what's bothering her—then this wife is responding in a childish way to adult problems that call for mature responses.

If her husband is an emotionally solid person, then he is sure to have difficulty dealing with his immature spouse. But with enough patience and the proper guidance, his wife could be helped by him. His maturity could possibly be the deciding factor that determines whether or not that marriage survives.

If, on the other hand, both spouses are equally irresponsible, then the relationship is surely in for rough times. Neither one of them will have the required maturity to control the strong feeling that they will inevitably feel. Both could predictably respond to each other in childish ways that are designed to hurt. Most of all, their responses would do nothing to help change things for the better. On the contrary, their childish solutions to some complex marital problems would most likely only serve to aggravate the situation and make matters worse.

What I am trying to say is that without a certain level of maturity, you cannot expect people to work out certain problems. It is just not possible. Good will and sincerity are not enough. If I come upon a victim of a heart attack who is lying in the street, I, of course, would like to save his life. If, however, I know nothing about heart attacks and what to do about them, chances are the man will die while I stand by wishing I could help.

In the same way, good will and sincere desire to solve certain marital problems are not nearly enough to do the job. There is a need to know what to do. But even that is hardly enough. It is necessary to have the right amount of good sense and courage that come with maturity to be able to carry out the actions the thinking mind is calling for.

Often, I am asked to help a couple in trouble with their marriage. It is clear to me what they must do to rectify their negative situation. And what is tragic is when I know that even if I could tell them all about it and make them see what they must do, they could do little to change anything because of their lack of maturity. One cannot give what one does not have. It's as simple as that!

INFIDELITY OF MAN

MAN IS NOT naturally monogamous. Men take more than one wife in many societies around the world. In our society, we insist that men keep only one mate. There are many who violate this law of our society (not to mention God's commandment), but they are instantly censured by society.

What I am trying to get across is that there are far too many married people who think that the wedding ceremony is an iron-clad guarantee of happiness forevermore. Of course, everybody knows that there are married people who don't get along together, quarrel all the time, and finally separate.

However, after having officiated at so many weddings, I maintain that few newlyweds even think of the possibility of a breakup.

It's not that I am a pessimist. On the contrary, I am an incurable optimist. I have to be to keep my sanity amidst all the problems that come my way every day. But I am a realist too. I have seen too much not to be.

Maybe it's because newlyweds just don't want to think about anything that might burst the romantic bubble. They would prefer to dream dreams of never-ending marital bliss.

I think a couple is only being intelligent to think about preserving their marriage. It prevents them from taking their love for granted.

And I have noted that whenever a couple on the threshold or separation comes to me with their conflicts, there has almost always been lots of "taking for granted" by both parties.'

I am trying to say that people in love should remain alert to any danger (internal as well as external) that might mean potential disaster. Their security should lie in the fact that they are constantly aware of and looking for danger signals. They should base their feelings of safety in the firm knowledge that when things are going well, they are in reality truly so.

So many women go into a state of stock when they discover that their husbands have mistresses. To hear them talk, you would think that they believed their husbands incapable of such a thing.

The truth of the matter is that men are very capable of infidelity. Given the right circumstances, the strongest can fall. Every man, whether single or married, is tempted daily. It doesn't matter how beautiful his wife or sweetheart is. Every male is attracted to women. God made them thus.

That a man is tempted or attracted is one thing. That he falls is something else again. If he is to keep his marriage or his courtship in one piece, he must remain vigilant.

She, on the other hand, should be understanding. She must not nag or show excessive jealousy when he opens up his heart to her.

Instead of getting depressed, she should see this as a warning signal of potential danger. She should then double her efforts to strengthen her husband in his moments of weakness.

If the wife is realistic enough to rise above the romantic bubble and remain alert to the possible dangers surrounding her marriage, she could very well avert marital disaster. And if her husband doesn't take things for granted, continued happiness is very much within his reach.

SATISFYING THE NEEDS OF EACH OTHER

THERE IS ONE reality that friends, lovers and married people find difficult to accept. That is that two people rarely have the capacity to satisfy all the needs of each other for a lifetime. It is so hard for a wife to admit that she is inadequate when it concerns the needs of the man she loves. It is undoubtedly very painful to face the fact that her husband will have to go elsewhere to fulfill some of his needs; that she cannot possibly be the answer to all his wants.

It is natural to desire to possess a loved one so completely that he becomes totally dependent on you. I said it was "natural". That does not mean it is a good thing. Let's be honest. An individual's needs, even only one person's, are so many and varied that one cannot ever be expected to answer all of them. This is just simply impossible. Thus, it is unrealistic to expect one's partner in marriage or a sweetheart to fulfill all our needs.

Many have relationships that end up on the rocks because of unrealistically high expectations that could never, even under the best circumstances, be realized. Young lovers, starry-eyed and blind to much of reality, who get into love and marriage expecting that they will be all to each other, are in for a rude awakening. They soon discover that nobody has a monopoly on good things; that God has spread His blessings all around the place so that we will be encouraged to interact with as many people as possible; and that unless they are willing to allow each other the freedom to seek additional fulfillment elsewhere, conflict will soon arise.

Watching a loved one go off to seek growth and satisfaction (I don't mean sexual satisfaction) that he believes is essential for his development is tough on anybody in love. It is unbearable for the person who is deeply insecure. The wife who feels that her marriage is shaky can experience only fear and apprehension when she sees her husband looking elsewhere to satisfy an important need. For example, if a plain and simple woman is married to a scientist, she will soon come to understand that her man has a need to interact with others who have the same interests. The need is less if she can understand his work and converse with him about it. Otherwise, she will have to give way and encourage him to seek out people who are familiar with the projects that are so important to him.

It takes humility, a feeling of genuine security and an authentic concern for the growth of the loved one to agree that you cannot answer to all of his needs. If you can admit this, sincerely and truly, chances are that your love is healthy. If not, I suggest you re-examine your relationship. It most likely is in need of some strengthening.

About the Author

BOB GARON was born in New Hampshire USA. He was sent to the Philippines in 1965 to do missionary work. He left the priesthood and received his dispensation from his vows in 1978. By being involved in organizations that addressed the needs of troubled youth, Bob built a name for himself and is known as the Father of the Therapeutic Community in Asia.

As a writer and columnist, he has written over 14,000 articles over the past four decades. He has helped and inspired countless individuals and couples through his live phone-in counseling on radio and television, as well as with motivational speaking.

Bob also set-up a management consultancy firm, and, together with his wife Emmy, founded the Golden Values Schools.

Up to his last days, Bob worked with people struggling to overcome various addictions and helped them get their lives back together. He passed away in 2021 at the age of 85.

Thank you for reading!

If you received value from this book, please consider leaving a review, however short, on the Amazon page. This will help get the message to others who may need or appreciate it.

Royalties earned from this book will help poor children in the Philippines get an education.

* * *

OTHER BOOKS WRITTEN BY BOB GARON

Loving is Living
Facing Life's Problems
Love & Courtship
Intimate Letters of Married Couples
Intimate Letters of Young Lovers
Reflections on Marriage

Made in the USA
Columbia, SC
26 November 2024